Simon M. Landis, Cyrus R. Morgan

A Full Account of the Trial of Simon M. Landis

Simon M. Landis, Cyrus R. Morgan

A Full Account of the Trial of Simon M. Landis

ISBN/EAN: 9783337816582

Printed in Europe, USA, Canada, Australia, Japan

Cover: Foto ©Suzi / pixelio.de

More available books at **www.hansebooks.com**

A FULL ACCOUNT

OF THE

TRIAL

OF

Simon M. Landis, M. D.

FOR

UTTERING AND PUBLISHING A BOOK ENTITLED

"SECRETS OF GENERATION."

———•••———

PHONOGRAPHICALLY REPORTED

By C. R. Morgan, M. D.

PUBLISHED BY

THE FIRST PROGRESSIVE CHRISTIAN CHURCH

PHILADELPHIA.

TRIAL

Before HON. WILLIAM S. PIERCE.

CHARLES GIBBONS, Esq.,

District Attorney.

JOHN G. MICHENER, Esq.,
DAMON Y. KILGORE, Esq.,

Counsel for Defendant.

Wednesday, January 12th, 1870.

The Grand Inquest, of the Commonwealth of Pennsylvania, inquiring for the city and county of Philadelphia upon their respective oaths and affirmations, do present, that

SIMON M. LANDIS,

late of the said county, yeoman on the twenty ninth day of December in the year of our Lord, one thousand eight hundred and sixty nine at the county aforesaid, and within the jurisdiction of this court, being a scandalous and evil disposed person, and contriving, devising and intending the morals as well of the youth as of other good citizens of this commonwealth to debauch and corrupt and to raise and create in their minds inordinate and lustful desires, with force and arms at Philadelphia aforesaid in the county aforesaid, unlawfully did utter, publish, sell and deliver to one S. F. Berneiser—a certain lewd wicked, scandalous, infamous, filthy and obscene printed book entitled, "Secrets of Generation," which said printed book is so lewd, filthy, wicked and obscene that the same would be offensive to the court here and improper to be placed upon the records thereof; wherefore the said Grand Inquest does not set forth the same in this indictment; to the manifest corruption and subversion of the youth and other good citizens of this Commonwealth, in their manners and conversation, in contempt of the laws of this Commonwealth, to the evil example of all others and contrary to the form of the act of the general assembly in such case made and provided, and against the peace and dignity of the Commonwealth of Pennsylvania.

So the Grand Inquest aforesaid upon the oaths and affirmations aforesaid do further present that the said SIMON M. LANDIS, of the said county, yeoman, as the day and year aforesaid, unlawfully and wantonly and maliciously did expose to and have for sale a certain lewd, filthy, wicked, scandalous and imfamous obscene printed book entitled the "SECRETS OF GENERATION," which said printed book is so lewd, filthy, wicked and obscene, that the same would be offensive to the court here and improper to be placed upon the records thereof, wherefore the said Grand Inquest does not set forth the same in this indictment, to the manifest corruption and subversion of the youth, and other good citizens of this Commonwealth in their manners and conversation, in contempt of the laws of this Commonwealth to the evil example of all others, and contrary to the form of the act of the General Assembly in such case made and provided and against the peace and dignity of the Commonwealth of Pennsylvania.

CHARLES GIBBONS, Dist. Att'y.

MR. GIBBONS.—Gentlemen of the Jury: —The Bill of Indictment which I am about to give you charges Simon M. Landis, with the uttering and publication of an obscene printed book, and also with exposing an obscene printed book for sale. This, gentlemen of the jury, is made an offence under our criminal code as follows :—

If any person shall publish or sell any filthy and obscene libel, or shall expose for sale, or exhibit for sale any indecent lewd and obscene print, painting or statuse, or if any person shall keep, maintain, any house, room, or gallery for the purpose of exposing, exhibiting any lewd, indecent obscene prints, pictures, paintings or statues and shall be convicted thereof such person shall be sen-

tenced to pay a fine not exceeding five hundred dollars, and undergo an imprisonment not exceeding one year.

A libel, gentlemen of the jury, is defined to be any malicious publication expressed either in print or in writing, or by signs, or by pictures tending to injure society at large, to defame the memory of the dead, or destroy the reputation of the living.

The publication of obscene printed matter was an offense at common law, and an indictable offense, and always has been. When I speak of common law, gentlemen, of the jury, I speak of time immemorial; it has been an indictable offense from time immemorial in that country from which we derive the most of our laws.

It was not incorporated into our criminal code until a few years ago, under the revision of the code made by the direction of the Legislature, although it was then an indictable offense at common law, and always has been in the State of Pennsylvania. It is an indictable offence under this statute which I have just read to you.

This bill of Indictment gentlemen, of the jury, charges that the offence consists in the sale, publication, or in the sale of a book entitled "THE SECRETS OF GENERATION," and the indictment sets forth that it is so lewd and filthy, and obscene that it is unfit to be spread upon the records of this court.

I shall proceed to lay before you, gentlemen of the jury, the evidence which will consist of the book itself. And I shall ask you to take that book to your room, to look at it for yourself, for you may very well imagine, if it is too obscene and lewd and filthy to be spread upon the records of the court it is too filthy and obscene to be read in the presence of a public audience.

Jury.

T. M. Lewis, Gentleman, 2145 Camac St.
Michael R. Tallman, Clerk, 309 Queen St.
Nicholas Rittenhouse, Gent. Ridge Road.
Charles Newkirk, Varnisher, 226 N. 4th St.
Joseph Fox, Manufacturer, 210 Green St.
Jacob Dixey, Pumpmaker, 1178 N. 13th St.
David Levzly, Merchant,——Green St.
David Bell, Cabinet Maker, 119 N. 17th St.

Wm. Farrel, Cabinet Maker, 225 Poplar St.
William H. Rice, Grocer, 1342 Ellsworth St.
James Warnick, Painter, 1735 Carpenter St.
John Krugg, Storekeeper, 1220 Germantown Avenue.

Witness for the Commonwealth.

Samuel F. Berneiser, Sworn.

Questions by MR. GIBBONS.

Q.—What is your occupation?

A.—Special Police Officer, attached to the detective service.

Q.—Do you know Simon M. Landis?

A.—Yes Sir.

Q.—Personally?

A.—I have known him for the neighborhood of twenty five years.

Q.—That is the man is it?

A.—Yes Sir.

Q.—Will you look at that book and state whether you ever saw it before?

A.—I have Sir.

Q—Where did you see it, Sir?

A.—I purchased this book, I saw it first in the hands of Dr. Landis and I purchased it from him.

Q.—Where was he when you saw him?

A.—In a building at the North West corner of Thirteenth Street and Girard Ave.

Q,—What kind of a building is it? Is it a store?

A.—No Sir, there was a printing office in part of the room and a lecture room in the middle, and in the back part, it seemed as if there was a private apartment, I was not in that.

Q.—You purchased that book of Defendant?

A.—Yes Sir.

Q.—Did you get anything else from him at the same time?

A.—Yes Sir, I purchased his "Sharp-Shooter," and "Sense and Nonsense," and he threw in the purchase his "Key to Heaven."

Paper offered in evidence, entitled "THE SHARP-SHOOTER"

MR. KILGORE.—He was not indicted for issuing a "SHARP-SHOOTER" or "KEY TO HEAVEN," and we object to this as not referring to the subject-matter for which he was indicted.

MR. GIBBONS.—I offer to show that this is

the "Sharp-Shooter" bought of Mr. Landis at the same time that the book was purchased, and that it is advertised for sale in this paper and thus to sustain our count that these books are for sale; and our count also that it was exposed for sale by Dr. Landis.

Mr. Kilgore.—We object to his bringing in a newspaper here, which is not mentioned in the indictment, as evidence of anything. If he bought a book he can give evidence of that fact. The fact that he bought some other paper or some other book not named in the indictment we think should have nothing to do with this charge.

Mr. Gibbons.—This paper was handed to the witness by Dr. Landis himself, and contains an advertisement of this identical book.

Objected to; overruled so far as it relates to the advertisement of the book in question.

Witness.—I received that paper from the hands of Dr. Landis.

Mr. Gibbons.—I offer the book in evidence called "The Secrets of Generation," *also*

The paper containing the advertisement of the book.

Mr. Kilgore.—I object to your offering that paper in evidence. According to your ruling, Your Honor, they have the right to put in evidence that part of the paper in which that book is advertised, but I question if they have the right to put in any other part.

Court.—All that I have ruled, is that it is evidence in that.

Mr. Kilgore.—The District Attorney may cut it out.

Mr. Gibbons.—We will give them the paper and they can read it.

Mr. Kilgore.—We have no objection to it if your Honor will instruct them to read simply the advertisement of that book, and have it marked for that purpose.

Court.—Let me see that. Hand that to the Jury and let them examine it for themselves.

Mr. Kilgore.—We object to its being offered now as we have not cross-examined the witness.

Cross-Examination, by Mr. Kilgore.

Q.—What is your name?

A.—Samuel F. Breneiser.

Q.—What is your business sir?

A.—I am at present a special police officer.

Q.—By whom appointed?

A.—By Daniel M. Fox.

Q.—Where do you do business?

A.—I report at the central police station.

Q.—What is your especial business as a police officer?

A.—I am detailed to have charge of the detective department at night.

Q.—You say you purchased this book of Dr. Landis. When?

A.—On the 29th ult.

Q.—What did you say to him when you called to purchase it?

A.—I asked him first for the "Sharp-Shooter," I then asked him for a copy of his "Sense and Nonsense," I told him there was another book that I wished. He told me he supposed it was the "Secrets of Generation," I told him yes.

Q.—You bought them?

A.—I did.

Q.—You paid for them?

A.—I did.

Q.—What did you pay for this book entitled "The Secrets of Generation?"

A.—I did not buy it singly, I paid for the whole lot.

Q.—What is the price of it?

A.—He informed me the price of that book was one dollar.

Q.—Did he tell you he did not sell it to minors?

A.—No Sir.

Q.—Well Sir, after you went to him to purchase that book, what did you next do?

A.—I went away.

Q.—Did you read these books?

A.—Part of them.

Q.—Did you read this book mentioned in the indictment?

A.—I read part of it, sir.

Q.—What part of it did you read, sir?

A.—If you will give me the book I will show it to you. [the book entitled "The Secrets of Generation" was shown to the witness] I read page 23 called, "How

4

to genera'e healthy and talented babies,"
and so on, up to page 28, "How to prevent
Conception," and page 28, from page 23 to
the balance of the book.

Q.—Now Sir why did you commence
at page 23?

Mr. GIBBONS.—I object.

Q.—Did you read that book by yourself
alone?

Mr. GIBBONS.—The only question is as
to whether he purchased the book, the
design is not to examine him as to the
contents of the book. All I have called
him for is to prove the purchase of the
book, the cross examination should be
confined to that point.

Mr. KILGORE.—I differ, with the District
Attorney, with regard to that last statement, I think we have a right to show by
this cross examination who this man is;
what credibility should attach to his testimony. I asked him the question if he
read the book alone and they object to it.
I insist it is a proper question and is
pertinent.

COURT.—In what way is it pertinent as to
the purchase of the book?

Mr. KILGORE.—It is pertinent in this way
it will show the animus, the intent of this
man in the purchase of this book.

COURT.—I do not see how it will show
that. Suppose he purchased this book
with the design of bringing this action, you
may ask him those questions direct.

Mr. KILGORE.—Well your Honor, if we
show by this examination that this man is
a mere tool in other parties' hands; that
he commenced this business for the purpose of black mail; have we the right to
ask this question?

COURT.—You can ask any question that
will affect the credibility of the witness. To
ask him how or where he read the book
does not affect his credibility, or the fact
that he purchased the book, or read it, I do
not see the pertinency.

Mr. KILGORE.-Usually your Honor, when
people read books they begin at the begin-
ing, but this man says he commenced at
the 23d page.

COURT.—What do you wish to show?

Mr. KILGORE.—It is pertinent to show

the object this man had in view in getting
this book.

COURT.—Very well, as touching that you
can show that.

Mr. KILGORE. If this was man actuated by
an unworthy motive, if it was not for the
public good, it bears directly upon his
character, as a witness.

COURT.—Put it in plain language, as to
what you intend to show by this witness.
If you show a mean motive, now tell
what the motive is.

Mr. KILGORE.—Black mail, and not to
benefit the public.

COURT.—Very well, it is admitted.

Q.—Now Sir, did you read that book,
in company or by yourself?

A.—I read it by myself, there was no
one near me.

COURT.—I ruled that question out in so
far as it stood, if it is for you to show any
corrupt motive, or levying black mail.

Q.—Who sent you to purchase this
book?

Objected to by Mr. Gibbons.

COURT.—I think this whole business can
be disposed of at once. The District Attorney had his attention drawn to it, as a
publication. He thought it was a case
which called the attention of the authority,
and Mr. Breneiser was, by authority of
the Court, brought here simply to testify as
to his agency. Now what may have been
his motive has nothing to do with the
question, in as much as this prosecution
is before the Court and Jury on authority
of the District Attorney.

Mr. KILGORE.— I asked of the witness,
Your Honor, who sent him to Dr. Landis,
to purchase that book.

Court—In what way is that material
I do not see the materiality of it.

Mr. KILGORE.—Your Honor this is a persecution. It is a conspiracy against this
defendant, and I propose to show by the
commonwealth's main witness, that he is
a party in it, and a party to it.

COURT.—What do you mean by a conspiracy?

Mr. KILGORE.—I mean by conspiracy that
it is an effort to get money out of this
defendant.

COURT.—Do you mean that it is an independent effort to levy black mail? Put any question that will tend to elicit that. If you mean a combination to persecute this man it is quite another question.

MR. KILGORE.—I do not mean that.

MR. GIBBONS.—I would like to ask him if his proposition is to prove that the authorities of the Commonwealth in bringing this prosecution have been influenced by corrupt motives.

MR. KILGORE—Not at all.

COURT.—Then if that is not the case I do not see what possible relevancy this question has. I understand this allegation to be that he is a party to levy black mail on Dr. Landis. Now you may put any question to elicit that.

Q.—Who sent you for that book, sir?

A.—I offered to go myself.

Q.—To whom?

A.—To parties with whom I was doing business.

Q.—Who are they?

A.—Parties connected with the detective service.

Q.—Name them, sir?

A.—I was doing business——

Q.—Will you answer my question?

A.—I was doing business with Messrs Cobb & Fletcher, any work that was given me to do.

COURT.—I think the true mode is first to ask him any questions touching any effort to levy black mail then to show who are the parties to that arrangement. It is evident that you are beginning at the other end. If you are not prepared to show such an effort made you had better abandon it.

MR. KILGORE.—It is possible, I do not understand how to bring this matter out. I think if I can approach it in this way I shall be more likely to get at the truth than if I commence at the other end.

COURT.—I suppose you have some knowledge of some facts. Now you can put some questions directly tending to elicit that fact. If not, you had better begin and confine your questions to sworn evidence.

MR. KILGORE.—As far as sworn evidence is concerned, I have none, but I have been told things which I believe to be true upon which those points are based.

Will Your Honor instruct this witness to give the names of those persons who sent him to buy that book?

COURT.—I think you had better begin at the other end and show an effort to levy black mail.

MR. KILGORE.—I wish to take the facts in order of time, to begin at the beginning. I simply asked who sent him and he has refused to answer.

COURT.—If you offer to follow this up with proof by facts showing the parties who sent him attempted to levy black mail it is pertinent, on the contrary if you are not prepared with facts, then I do not think it is revelant.

MR. KILGORE.—Your Honor, if we do not show that, I am willing the whole matter should be stricken out.

COURT.—That consumes a large amount of time and goes into a matter of relevancy.

Q.—Will you give me the names of those who sent you?

MR. GIBBONS.—May it please your Honor as the counsel does not seem to feel disposed to act upon the suggestion of the court I beg leave to present you the consideration of this single point. This prosecution has been commenced by the representative of the Commonwealth as a matter of public duty. He produces here a witness upon the stand who purchased this book which is offered in evidence, the obscene book mentioned in the indictment. The witness has been interrogated on the part of the prosecution upon a single point alone and the only question that can possibly come before the jury so far as this book is concerned, is, first, whether this book was purchased from Dr. Landis and secondly whether the book is an obscene book. If the jury find these two facts they must convict the defendant. Now can it make the slightest difference to this prosecution or to the defendant in this prosecution, whether this book was purchased from him by a personal friend or a personal enemy, can it make any possible difference whether the witness upon the stand, with other Police Officers combined if you choose to obtain this book from Dr. Landis for an unworthy purpose, or not, the fact that he did sell this book, and this man did obtain it for some purpose, no matter what purpose, coming to the knowledge of the prosecuting officers of the Commonwealth, this bill of indictment, founded upon the facts in evidence, is found and presented by the Grand Jury. Now if any persons have unlawfully or maliciously entered upon a conspiracy to wrong this man he has remedy at law. It certainly does not affect the issue in this present case. Now, I beg your Honor to confine the cross-examination of this witness in this case to the points on which he was interrogated, in his examination in chief. If it be a defence that there was a conspiracy and your Honor thinks there was a conspiracy, let them introduce it in the regular way and not in a cross-examination of the witness produced by the Commonwealth.

Mr. Kilgore.—Your Honor, I am very much opposed to these arguments because they consume valuable time. I have an important case in the Supreme Court and am very anxious to get through with this case but, Sir, I must insist upon all the rights of this defendant under the law of the land. There is another question involved, other than that to which the District Attorney alluded, and if we can show that this witness engaged in this prosecution for the purpose of persecution, or for the purpose of levying black mail upon the defendant, it will go directly to his character, with this Jury as to his credibility.

Court.—That I think, and therefore I said you may ask him any question which tended to that effect, but merely asking him these few questions unless you intend to follow it and prove it has been done for an unlawful purpose.———

Mr. Kilgore.—Your Honor, I propose, not only to show, who sent him, who were in league with him, but that he went at an improper time, did his work in the basest manner possible. That he did it not as an officer of the law, for the public good, but for the sole purpose of putting down, crushing and making money out of a man, who belived that he was doing God's service. That is why I ask this question and why I propose to follow it up with others involving the credibility of this witness.

Court.—Now if you can show what that manner was, and show some connection between the matters proposed to be shown by him, you can go on asking what they were.

Mr. Kilgore.—Cheerfully, Your Honor.

Q.—When did you make affidavit in reference to the purchase of this book? On what day?

A.—Last Saturday a week.

Q.—Before what magistrate.

A.—Before the Clerk of the Police Magistrate Kerr, Central Station.

Q.—What time in the day did you get the warrant?

A.—I did not get any warrant.

Q.—Did you arrest this defendant?

A.—No sir.

Q.—Did you go with the men who did arrest him?

A.—I went with parties up to the Hall.

Q.—At the time that he was arrested?

A.—Yes sir.

Q.—Did you see him arrested?

A.—I seen him coming out of the Hall.

Q.—Did you point him out to the persons who had the warrant?

A.—No sir.

Q.—Who had the warrant?

A.—Messers Cobb & Fletcher, I understood had it, I did not see it in their hands.

Q.—Where was you when they arrested him?

A.—When I went into the Hall they were coming out.

Q.—At what time?

A.—I suppose it was in the neighborhood of seven o'clock.

Mr. Kilgore.—I do not want any of your supposings. About what time was it according to your best knowledge and recollection?

A.—According to my best knowledge and recollection it was seven o'clock in the evening sir.

Q.—It was sunday night?

A.—Yes sir.

Q—Did you know sir that Dr. Landis was to preach in that Hall, Fifth and Callowhill Streets on that evening?

A.—I had understood that he was.

Q.—You knew that fact before you made this arrest?

A.—I did not make any arrest.

Q.—Why did you take him at that time?

A.—I did not arrest him.

COURT.—Is it pertinent to the facts that you should ask him all these questions?

MR. KILGORE.—I think it is your Honor. I do not mean to ask a question that does not bear directly upon the main points at issue, and if I do not show that they have a very important bearing, I will never ask your Honor to take my word again.

COURT.—It was near seven o'clock, at the time he was giving an address in Harmonial Hall.

MR. KILGORE.—He was going to preach a sermon, but not in Harmonial Hall.

Q.—Had the people commenced to gather there?

A.—There were some people assembled in the Hall.

Q.—Where did you take him?

A.—I had nothing to do with him.

COURT.—Is the question about malicious arrest, or the publication of a book?

MR. KILGORE.—This *is* a malicious arrest. I think the question pertinent.

COURT.—I do not care what motive prompted the arrest for the publication of this book unless you can show that the arrest was made with a view to some unlawful design, it does not matter whether the arrested person was taken out of bed or in the midst of the preaching of a sermon or attending church or elsewhere.

MR. KILGORE.—For the benefit of the Commonwealth's officer I will say that we shall take the broad ground that this book is not obscene, that it is a privileged publication, that it is a scientific work, that it is just such a work that every father ought to put into the hands of his adult children.

COURT.—That is another thing, you can argue that when the book is before you.

MR. KILGORE.—Now I propose to show how this defendant was treated by this man who is on the stand, and his associates, in order to black mail this defendant, that is my design.

COURT.—Give us the fact and show that design. I suppose it is unfortunate for a

man to be arrested under any circumstances, any where in his house, at home or at church, the mere fact of his arrest does not alter the case.

MR. KILGORE.—Now we propose to show that Doctor Landis was taken to the Central Station, that he was locked up in a felons cell, that he was kept there until morning with no opportunity of communicating with his counsel or friends, that bail was refused him——

COURT.—I told you that is not pertinent at this time. You have a right if you have been abused, to recover by legal process for that abuse. There is a remedy for all these things. You can have a right for trial in the civil or criminal court, but that question does not arise here now, the question now is, was this book purchased and published by the Doctor, the defendant? 2d. If so is it an obscene book? That is the question now. All the matters for law are open for you to prove.

MR. KILGORE.—Does your Honor decide that I cannot show the mode of the arrest, what was done at the time and show this man's connection with it and why he should not be regarded as a credible witness?

COURT.—You can show that by this witness in order to show the bias of his mind.

Q.—Why did you go after this book. What design had you in view by its purchase?

COURT.—I do not see that has anything to do with it. It does not show any act or intent or any act done by him.

The fact this witness purchased the book and that his mind was therefore in a certain biased condition would not affect his credibility or if he was biased by prejudice against the defendant by what others may have done or any oppression defendant suffered at the hands of the witness does not interfere in any manner as touching the main question or as touching the credibility of the witness.

Q.—When Doctor Landis was brought before a magistrate did you testify against him?

A.—I testified that I purchased this book.

Q.—Did you say upon the trial that you had never read this book?

A.—No, Sir. I told them I read part of it.

Q.—Has the book demoralized you, sir? Objected to.

Q.—Is there anything obscene in that book?

Objected to, and withdrawn.

Q.—Do you know anything with reference to this man being confined in cell number one at the Central Station?

COURT.—I do not see what that has to do with the question.

MR. KILGORE.—I wish your Honor would instruct this witness to remain in court.

MR. GIBBONS.—I have marked some of the particular passages here, gentlemen of the jury, to which I will ask your attention when you retire to your room. I offer in evidence this advertisement of the book contained in this newspaper. It is a newspaper which appears to be regularly published. The "Sharp Shooter," price five cents.

MR. KILGORE.—I object to all, your Honor, except the advertisement.

Commonwealth Closed.

Opening by Mr. Michener.

GENTLEMEN OF THE JURY.—It becomes my lot as one of the counsel for the defendant to lay before you the line of defence that we expect to take. He has been indicted and brought in here for trial before you, gentlemen, under the charge of writing and publishing an obscene libel. It is not set forth in the indictment—this book itself; but is referred to, as stated by the District Attorney, as too filthy and obscene to be put upon the records of this Court. This it seems to me is pre-judging the publication itself. We shall take the ground of defense here, gentlemen, that this book was written and published by a practising physician; that it was done upon scientific grounds; that he believed, as a physician, from the large amount of experience that he had had, that some work of this description became absolutely necessary for the assistance of the human family; that it is purely a scientific work; that it does not come within the class of publications that the law calls obscene; and too filthy to set forth in the bill of indictment to be placed upon the rcords of the Court. We know very well or at least we have reason to believe, we who are not medical men, that in order to examine the human body, in order to be prepared to assist the unfortunate, that it becomes necessary for an exposure of ever part of the human system, and in that exposure to the medical student and to the physician himself it becomes necessary, in order to give information to others that it should be set forth so as to be printed, I may say to you that we will bring a large number of medical gentlemen who will state that this book is not in their view an obscene and filthy publication but that it is a scientific medical work published not with malicious views that makes a crime or with the motive of reaching the sensual appetite and causing the public to come forth and buy the book, hat he who published it might make the paltry sum of one dollar upon each copy sold. No, gentlemen, though there are obscene passages in this book perhaps under certain circumstances and under certain views, yet, I say, in the hands of the scientific man, or placed in the hands of any gentleman of the jury who is a member of the community, or in the hands of his wife to read with a view to receiving information, in order to protect the human system, from the injuries that arise from the careless communications between the sexes, this book is not an obscene and filthy book. We believe that we shall show to you, that we have witnesses here in court who have been benefited by it. We are in an age of the world in which many medical men have felt and expressed themselves to the effect that in order to the protection of the human family information was necessary to be given to them upon these very subjects. A physician of high standing in the city of Boston, Mass., not perhaps in the line of this publication, has put forth a little book called "Why not" upon a subject of deep interest at this time to the whole community. It relates to the female population getting rid of the labor of bearing offspring and raising them up, called abortion in its early stages. Dr. Storer with many other physicians believing that it was injuring the sexual organs and that it was a sin before God practised by a large portion of this community, puts forth this book. It is laid before the Medical Association of the United States it not only received their approval, but they award to him the gold medal. The subject can be treated of by him in this little book and in a way which may be regarded as to a very serious extent obscene, if spoken of in the family circle or in the drawing room.

It is believed that that book has been very beneficial to the community, so much so that he has just published and has now for sale at the various leading bookstores in this city a work called "Why Is It" a work addressed to the male portion of the population upon the same subject. We say to you, gentlemen, then, that this publication of ours was issued with the same motive over the name of Dr. Landis as you will see when you read the title page, not put forth secretly in order to sell the book upon the street without regard to the morals of the community, but entered in the District Court of the United States for the Eastern District of Pennsylvania and sold by him as a physician, intended for the use of the adult population.

I think if we succeed in showing to you that Dr. Landis is a physician; that he is in considerable practice here, perhaps an extensive practice, I do not know to what extent; if we succeed in bringing before you medical gentlemen of high standing who say they have read this book, and that they regard it as a scientific publication and that the motive of its publication was for the benefit of the human family and that they believe many persons have b·en benefitted in the circle of this practice by it, I think you will agree with me that it is no' obscene. I have been informed since I have been engaged in this case that there are various books sold here in secret. We do not come within this class of publications; we publish openly; and we sell openly in connection with our practice, led to it by the many cases of injuries brought before us and the impropriety of the conduct of the parties in this connection. Now I think gentlemen, if we succeed in doing that, that you must acquit the defendant; you must find that his motive was that of a scientific man with a view of benefitting the human family, whatever the book may be. If it is ten times worse than that which is set forth, and you find that he is a scientific man, a physician of high standing, and the book is published with the intent to benefit the human family yon cannot convict the defendant. You must put it upon the other ground that this book belongs to the Fanny Hill publications which pander to the sensual appetite and injure the rising generation; but his motive was the selling the book for a beneficial end; but if you find that his motive was to sell the book to make money you will convict him, and his Honor upon the bench convinced by you that that is a fact will give him the whole penalty of the law. I think we shall be able to clearly satisfy you that there was no criminal motive and to satisfy His Honor upon the bench who will look carefully into this matter and deliver the charge to you when we have closed. I think that we will be able to show to you by our medical testimony that it seems to have become necessary that this character of information should be conveyed to the adult members of the community; that there has been so much carelessness and as this book says so much beastly behavior among a large portion of the male community, that some information is necessary upon that subject just as it was supposed by Dr. Storer and printed by him and presented to the Medical Association of the United States, that it should bring home to every family the impropriety of destroying the foetus at an early state of conception injuring the individual, destroying their constitution and preventing us from having the population God intended us to have.

We shall endeavor to show to you by our medical testimony that a large amount of disease is caused by impropriety in these matters, by the want of knowledge; that it was necessary that this publication should be made and that its intent is to guard the people before it becomes too late; to guard them against those injuries that produce diseases before they require a medical adviser. There is no other way to reach it than by scientific, medical publications that can be placed in the hands of individuals. Large medical publications are expensive and thus out of their reach.

We can show to you, if we are permitted to do so, London Publications of the first standing containing the very things that are objected to in this publication.

Gentlemen we will lay our testimony before you.

[Diploma offered in evidence dated 12th. February 1853, Eclectic Medical College Philadelphia.]

MR. KILGORE.—We propose to prove by all these witnesses, that this book is not an obscene book ; that Dr. Landis is a practising physician in good standing in Philadelphia; that his character for purity and morality is unimpeachable. We propose to prove by this witness, and several others that the information conveyed in this book is valuable ; and that the world needs it, and the sufferings of women demand it.

Testimony for the Defence.

Dr. *Joseph Longshore*, affirmed.

MR. KILGORE.—Do you know Dr. Landis?

A.—Yes Sir.

Q.—How long have you known him ?

A.—Ten or twelve years.

Q.—You are a practising Physician ?

A.—Yes sir, for about fifteen years.

Q.—Do you know others who know him ?

A.—Yes Sir.

Q.—What is his character for morality ?

A.—I never heard it called in question.

Q.—Or for virtue and purity ?

A.—I never heard it questioned.

Q.—Is there a direct communication between the brain and the genital organs of the human body?

Objected to as irrelevant, to the character of Dr. Landis.

MR. KILGORE.—I have got through with that.

MR. GIBBONS.—I do not see what that has to do with the question.

MR. KILGORE.—I could not be more astonished than to hear such a statement from the District Attorney. I am surprised that the gentleman does not know, we said we proposed to show that the information, that this book conveyed, was necessary to the community in which we live, rendered necessary by ignorance of these laws and the diseases which are the result of ignorance on the part of married people to whom this book is addressed. I hope it will not be necessary to say anything further. We propose to show that this book is a scientific and medical book, and have prepared questions in order to substantiate that fact, and others, based upon science, and upon truth which science has demonstrated within the last few years. The question " Is there a direct communication between the brain and the genital organs " is the one to which objection is made. On the page marked by the Dist. Attorney, Dr. Landis has given proper information to married people in reference to the laws of nature, in generation, how to generate a race of men and women, that will be beautiful, healthful and pure, instead of the criminals and diseased persons, three-fourths of whom die, before attaining to adult age. Dr. Landis shows his fellow-men how to commence. And I wish to show that the instruction given respecting this very act of commencement, by which a new human soul is generated, which none but ignorant or obscene persons will make fun of, or treat lightly, is, an important part of the information given in this book. And also that the instruction is in accordance with natures laws, and beneficial to society, in the highest degree. I ask leave, your Honor, in these questions, to show these facts, because I believe them vital to this case.

Q—Now will you please answer my questions ?

COURT.—I do not think it is admissible.

MR. KILGORE.—Is that your decision ?

COURT.—The question is not admissible.

MR. KILGORE.—Will your Honor note an exception. I offered this question to show that this information is in strict accordance with science and with natural laws and in order to prevent those diseases with which this defendant has come in contact, and in order to show how those diseases might be prevented, by understanding the proper conditions of mind and body in order to properly generate a pure and healthy child. If your Honor rules this out, I wish to except to this ruling.

COURT.—Very well, I rule it out.

MR. KILGORE.—I now ask. What are the uses of the genital organs?

Objected to, and ruled out.

MR. KILGORE.—I will ask another question

MR. GIBBONS.—I object to all these questions. This book which is given in evidence is a strictly private book to married persons on the secrets of generation.

MR. KILGORE.—This man is charged with being a criminal, and he is brought here to be tried because he has written this book which goes into the philosophy of the highest use of the genital organs which is " Procreation." He has given us instruction which will prevent disease and produce healthy, moral, and holy offspring. For that he is brought into this Court as a criminal. I asked these questions to show that this book is based upon a right view of this subject; that it is correct in science and in its deductions; that the information, if practised as he has laid down in his book, which they have branded as obscene, would result beneficially to all those who would obey its teachings.

I propose to show by these witnesses that in the moment of generation of a human being the condition of the mother gives character, for all time, to that immortal being, and that it is of the utmost importance that Nature's law be not violated; that a knowledge of Nature's law on this subject does not convey impurity to the mind, but obedience thereto the highest purity, and the highest and holiest expression of love on earth for all men and women. To the pure all things are pure. A right use of all things made by the hands of the Divine Being promote purity, while impurity and obscenity consist in the abuse. I propose to show that there are several diseases of which this———

COURT.—If you will direct your argument to the point of relevancy I shall be very happy to hear from you. The question is whether this is an obscene book.

MR. KILGORE.—That is exactly what we propose to offer in proof. I propose to do it in a scientific and strictly proper manner. We propose to show also that the law sustains us in the position which we have taken. The law says: *If the use to be attained is justifiable, or if the object is to give information to the community, to those who have a right and ought to know, in order that they may obtain such information, the occasion is lawful, and the party may then justify or excuse the publication,* and it says this, your Honor, when the book is really objectionable on account of the language used. If your Honor notice in these questions I have commenced at the beginning, and have followed it up in reference to the very cases which these physicians are called upon to treat, and especially which this defendant was called upon to treat, and being moved by the sufferings of his patients, he was constrained to write this information for the community in order to prevent these diseases. This is why we propose to bring in this testimony. I deem this testimony of vital importance to the defendant, to the District Attorney, to this Court, these jurors, and to every person within the sound of my voice, and all whom these words may reach, to the administration of public justice, and the good of those who will come after us. I know that it will take less time than to come at this information in any other way.

COURT.—I think they are not admissible.

MR. KILGORE.—I take an exception to your Honor's ruling.

Q.—Have you read this book entitled "The Secrets of Generation," Doctor?

A.—No Sir.

Q.—Have you read any parts of it?

A.—I read parts of the 25th and 26th pages.

Q.—Those pages which are marked?

A.—The parts I read are marked, Sir.

Q.—Well now, Doctor, do you consider that obscene?

MR. GIBBONS.—I object to that. That is

a question for the jury. I do not suppose there are any experts in obscenity.

Mr. Kilgore.—If Your Honor please, I offer to prove by this physician who has practised a life-time in this profession, who has to do with both sexes and who ought to know in reference to the question whether this medical work is obscene or not obscene. I offer to prove by this witness that this book is not an obscene book, and as a medical expert I offer his testimony. I do not know who would be regarded as an expert in the mind of the District Attorney, I think we have the right to call medical gentlemen who have to do with these diseases and with works which are published for the sake of giving information upon these subjects. I wish to show by this gentleman and by all who follow him that this book is a medical but not an obscene book.

Court.—I think the fact of its obscenity will manifest itself to any one and it is not necessary to call an expert to prove that and I overrule the offer to show such a fact.

Mr. Kilgore.—Will Your Honor note an exception to that ruling.

Court.—Yes sir.

Q.—Do you regard this book as a scientific book?

Objected to on account of the fact that a scientific book may be a very obscene book.

Q.—Is that a scientific and medical book?

Objected to.

Q.—Is that a medical book?

Objected to.

Court.—You have no right to ask whether it is a medical book or otherwise.

Mr. Kilgore.—I offer Dr. Longshore to prove that this book is a medical book written upon strictly scientific principles as far as medical science goes and we wish to show that it is beneficial to society and its teaching true.

Court.—It may be true, and it may be a very obscene book.

Mr. Kilgore.—Undoubtedly, I wish to show that the law privileges this book, because it is strictly a scientific and a medical work. Then I submit that this question is pertinent. We have a right to show that it is such from the position we take under the law of the land.

Mr. Gibbons.—I object to your showing it.

Court.— It is overruled.

Mr. Kilgore.—will Your Honor note an exception?

Q.—In Medical works, treating upon these subjects, is it customary to put plates in them showing the genial organs of both Sexes?

Objected to as irrevalent and ruled out.

Q.—Have you known Dr. Landis as a practitioner of medicine?

A.—I have known him by reputation as a practitioner of medicine, I am not intimately acquainted with the gentlemen. I have seen him many times.

Q.—Do you think the information contained in this book is needed by the public?

Objected to, ruled out and an exception taken.

Q.—In your practice, Doctor, are there many diseases which you have to treat occasioned by the ignorance of men and women in the marriage relation?

Objected to.

Mr. Gibbons.—No doubt the case is so, I object to it as it has nothing whatever to do with the question.

Mr. Kilgore.—Well now, Your Honor if we can do nothing in this case but to show the character of this Defendant, we might as well join the District Attorney and ask the Jury to convict this defendant at once.

Court.—He need not be convicted if the book does not convict him.

Mr. Kilgore.—We wish to show that the book does not convict him and offer to show that is no more objectionable than other medical works at large in the community, that are not considered obscene, and that are sold everywhere, even at auctions, that is what we propose to prove. The question is shall we have the privilege.

Court.—Suppose there are fifty books, that does not affect the question or justify the publication of this book, if it is an improper book.

Mr. Kilgore.—I grant Your Honor, but I wish to show this by medical men, and to bring in the decisions of the courts in reference to medical works which are privileged and against which actions have been brought—which have been dismissed because they were *privileged.* That is why I offer this testimony. If we cannot get the testimony in, I do not see how we can go on with this case. I can show this to be the law by the authorities.

COURT.—The positions which you have laid down are very correct. For *instance* in order to illustrate, we all know it is necessary to view the human body in all its parts, for diseases of various kinds, by physicians, eminently proper required by medical science. What then? Why they should be properly treated under proper circumstances. You may do it before a clinic class, you may do it in a private chamber, but nobody would contend, that this thing ought to be brought into a court-house, and there done, or taken upon the highway, and there expose the human person. Some things are proper to be done in secret, and others to be public. A publication of a medical character may properly be admitted to a class of students which certainly cannot be produced upon the public highway. It would then be obscene. In their places they are necessary to the scientific. It is the motive; it is the peculiar circumstances in the case upon which the case itself must be determined.

MR. KILGORE.—That is just what we wish to show.

COURT.—Now if it were shown that Dr. Landis was publishing these things anywhere to the injury of the morals of the town, then he would be guilty of an offence of obscene exposure and yet if it were done in a close room or done in the private chamber of a patient, which would be eminently proper, therefore, gentlemen, if this man does these things this way as a physician, it is unquestionably correct. But when a man does these things openly and publicly, which when done privately are not obscene, then they become incorrect and cannot be justified.

MR. KILGORE.—If Your Honor please this book is a "STRICTLY PRIVATE BOOK FOR MARRIED PERSONS," which says also on the title

page of the book, "THIS BOOK MUST NOT LIE ABOUT THE HOUSE, *but every male and female should read it.*" We propose to show that not one of these books has been for sale to everybody like other medical works which are ten times as objectionable as this book, some of them in auction rooms in this city, at public sales, even. Dr. Landis has sold this book himself, and to adult persons only. He put the price at one dollar for the very purpose of making it cost too much for children to purchase. He has kept these books under his own control. I propose to prove all this by several witnesses.

COURT.—Then your offer is not in order.

MR. KILGORE.—Please note an exception. I propose to show that this is the law; that the law will not presume malice in this case but on the other hand it will presume the innocence of the defendant. His malice must be shown by evidence.

We propose to show further, that this man has sacrificed more than five thousand dollars, during the last twelve months in this cause. That he is at this present moment not worth a hundred dollars, although he has an income of six thousand dollars from his practice, but that he gives nearly all of it for the reformation of the people, believing that in this way he is doing God's service, and following the example of the meek and lowly, but crucified Jesus.

Now Sir, If we can show that this book is a proper book to circulate——

MR. GIBBONS.—Show the book to the jury and let them say.

COURT.—I don't think it is a question for experts at all, every man is a judge.

Q.—Is this information proper to be given to the public by a physician?

MR. GIBBONS.—That has been ruled out sir.

COURT.—Ruled out as a question for the jury.

Q.—Do you know Dr. Landis to be a regular physician?

MR. GIBBONS.—You have proved that by his certificate.

Q.—Do you know of similar works, published by physicians in regular standing?

Objected to as having been previously ruled out.

Mr. Kilgore.—I understood the District Attorney to assume the responsibility of this prosecution?

Mr. Gibbons.—I do sir, as the Officer of the Commonwealth in my official capacity.

Mr. Kilgore.—[To the witness.] Do you think the information contained in this book should be confined only to colleges?

Objected to as being the same question given in another form.

Q.—Do you think the world is suffering in consequence of a lack of the very information which is found in this book?

Court.—That is a question for the jury to determine.

Q.—In your practice have you had occasion to treat females for diseases, which have been caused in consequence of the ignorance of their husbands on the subjects treated in this book?

Objected to.

Q.—Is that what you would call a book under seal?

Objected to.

Court.—A book under seal of secrecy.

Mr. Gibbons.—I do not care what the Doctor calls it, it makes no difference.

Mr. Kilgore.—That will do Doctor. They do not want the truth.

———

Robert Hall sworn.—

Mr. Kilgore.—You know Dr. Landis?

A.—Yes sir.

Q—How long have you known him?

A.—About eight or ten years.

Q.—Is he your family physician?

A.—Yes sir.

Q.—Has been?

A.—Yes sir.

Q.—Do you know others that know him.

A.—Yes sir.

A.—If you are intimately acquainted with him, what is his character for purity?

A.—Very good.

Q.—Do you know anything of this work called "The Secrets of Generation."

A.—I have never read it, I have heard of it.

No Cross Examination.

———

Lloyd Evans sworn.

Mr. Kilgore.—Do you know Dr. Landis?

A.—I do sir.

Q—How long have you known him

A.—About five years.

Q.—You know others who know him?

A.—I do.

Q.—What is his character, and reputation among those who know him, for purity?

A.—Very excellent, sir, a very proper citizen I should presume.

Q.—Has he been your physician, sir?

A.—He has.

Cross Examined.

Mr. Gibbons.—Who have you heard speak of his character as a man of purity?

Mr. Kilgore.—One moment before you cross-examine. [To the witness.] Do you know anything of his sacrificing his money freely for this reformation?

Objected to and overruled as irrevalent.

Mr. Kilgore.—Now sir, the law is plain, that if this man has written an obscene book in the opinion of these twelve men, and they think he did it with a good motive, to benefit the community, (and we shall ask your Honor to so charge the jury) they cannot convict him. We offer to show that this man did not write this book for the purpose of making money; but on the other hand, that he gives all his income for the dissemination of these truths he conceives necessary for the benefit of society.

Court.—That is your own opinion. If he should set fire to your house do you think I should instruct the jury to acquit because he did it for the benefit of society?

Mr. Kilgore. — I think your Honor should so instruct them.

Court.—I have the decision of the Supreme Court on that point, sir.

Mr. Kilgore.—I propose to show the authority to so charge the jury.

Court.—Unless he pleads to insanity. If you put that plea in——

Mr. Kilgore.—We do not put that plea in at all, your Honor.

Court.—There is no other way I can see.

Mr. Kilgore.—Do you know what Dr

Landis' objects were in publishing and circulating this book ?

Objected to.

Cross Examination.

Mr. Gibbons.—Who did you ever hear speak of Dr. Landis' character as a man of purity ?

A.—Various members of our church.

Q.—Name some of them.

A.—Mr. Hall.

Q.—What is his first name?

A.—Robert Hall.

Q —What church is he a member of?

A.—The First Progressive Christian Church of Philadelphia, Dr. Landis pastor.

Q —You are one of his congregation, then, are you?

A.—I am Sir.

Q.—The First · Progressive Christian Church? Is that known as a free love church?

Mr. Kilgore.—I have no objection to the answer, but I say the question is an improper one and should not be asked. It is an insult to the witness.

A.—I do not understand the question as to what free love means.

Mr. Gibbons.—If you do not understand it I will not undertake to explain it to you.

Q —You have heard Mr. Hall say he was a man of purity, when?

A.—I cannot say the day.

Q.—Was it within a week ?

A.—It was.

Q —Since the arrest ?

A.—Yes sir, and before also.

Q.—How long before ?

A.—Well probably for years, occasionally.

Q.—Was his character as a man of purity, under discussion at the time.

A.—No sir, not under discussion, merely mentioned in the course of conversation, I presume.

Q.—Will you please to state under what circumstances he said he was a man of purity?

A.—I cannot say exactly.

Q.—Who was present when it was said?

A.—There was nobody but ourselves.

Q.—Who ?

A.—Mr. Hall and myself, at his house.

Q.—At whose house ?

A.—At Mr. Hall's house ?

Q.—Now was this since the commencement of this prosecution, the occasion to which you now refer ?

A.—It was.

A.—Did you ever hear anybody else say he was a man of purity of character?

A.—I cannot remember of any.

Q.—Then how can you say to this jury upon your oath that his reputation is that of a man of purity of character ?

A.—By my knowledge of the man—by being associated with him.

Q.—Then you only know from your own experience and from intercourse with the man himself?

A.—Yes sir.

Q.—From that you infer his general character is that of purity ?

A.—Yes sir.

Redirect Examination.

Mr. Kilgore.—Do you not know that Dr. Landis is regarded by the whole congregation to be a pure man ?

Objected to as a leading question, and that he has already stated his means of knowledge.

Court.—He said he never heard any one speak of it but Mr. Hall.

Mr. Kilgore —Very well, I will change my question. Do you know the estimate in which Dr. Landis is held by his congregation as a moral Christian minister ?

Objected to.

Court.—What is his general character for purity ? Did you ever hear it questioned by any member of his congregation ?

A.—I did not.

Mr. Kilgore.—Is his congregation a very large one ?

A.—What would you call a large one ?

Q.—How many persons go to hear him preach ?

A.—On Sunday night I judge there must have been a thousand.

Q.—Is it usual for him to have as many as that ?

A.—It is when he has a large hall for their accommodation. When he preaches in a small hall he preaches to smaller congregations.

Charles Wagner sworn.

MR. KILGORE.—You know Dr. Landis?

A.—Yes sir.

Q.—How long have you known him?

A.—Eight or nine years.

Q.—Have you known him intimately?

A.—Yes sir.

Q.—Do you know others who know him?

A.—Yes sir.

Q.—What is his character for purity as a man and as a minister?

MR. GIBBONS.—We object to his character as a minister, that is not involved.

Q—Well, is he a pastor of the First Progressive Church?

A.—Yes sir.

Q.- Does a large congregation attend there usually?

A.—Yes sir.

Q.—Do you know a large number of people who know Dr. Landis?

A.—Yes sir.

Q.—He is an outspoken man is he?

A.—Yes sir.

Q.—He is not a man likely to conceal his motives.

A.—No sir.

Objected to as a matter that has nothing to do with his book.

MR. KILGORE.—I think if our friends will object less, they would get at the truth faster. I wish to know his reputation for purity.

COURT.—You must confine your remarks to character.

MR. KILGORE.—We can prove that by no witness. There is no human being who can testify to your Honor's character for purity. The character is beyond the ken of of any human being. Reputation is what others think of you, character is what you are. I will withdraw that question.

Q.—Did you ever hear Dr. Landis' character for purity questioned by any person of respectable character in Philadelphia?

Objected to.

Q.—What is his genuine character for purity?

A.—As far as I know it is good.

Q.—Did you ever hear it called in question?

MR. GIBBONS.—We object to that as opening the door to show cases of immorality.

Cross Examination.

Q.—When did you hear his character for purity spoken of?

A.—Since the arrest, and I have heard before that.

Q.—Who spoke of it?

A.—A friend of mine.

Q.—Please to name him sir.

A.—William Ahles.

Q.—When was it spoken of by William Ahles?

A.—A short time past.

Q.—When?

A.—I could not tell how long ago.

Q.—When?

A.—Five or six years ago.

Q.—When was it last spoken of to you by Mr. Ahles?

A.—Not lately, I have not seen him lately.

Q—When did you last see him sir, how long ago?

A.—I saw him last Sunday.

Q.—Did not he speak of it then?

A.—No sir.

Q.—You have not heard William Ahles, speak of it for a long time, have you?

A.—Yes sir.

Q.—Can you name any other person?

A.—A young lady, a friend of mine.

Q.—Who was the young lady?

A.—Miss Amber.

Q.—When did she speak of it?

A.—Since the arrest.

Q.—Any body else?

A.—No.

Q.—Where did Miss Amber speak of it?

A.—At my house.

Q.—All the persons whom you have heard speak of the character of Dr. Landis for purity, are Miss Amber and William Ahles?

A.—Yes sir.

Q.—These are the only persons?

A.—Yes sir,

———

Dr. Mincer, affirmed by the uplifted hand.

MR. KILGORE.—Do you know the defendant?

A.—I do sir.

Q.—How long have you known him?

A.—I think about seventeen years.

Q.—Do you know others who know him?

A.—Yes sir, I do.

Q.—What is his reputation and general character for purity?

A.—I have never heard it questioned.

Q.—Have you been accustomed to listen to his lectures?

A.—No sir, nor have I ever seen his book except in court.

Q.—You have read this paragraph, the one that is marked?

A.—Yes sir.

Cross Examination.

MR. GIBBONS.—I understand you to say you never heard anything said about his character for purity?

A.—I will state what he stated to me some seventeen years ago.——

MR. GIBBONS.—That is not evidence.

Redirect Examination.

MR. KILGORE.—The District Attorney, did not quote you quite right, you stated that you had never heard his character quesnoned. Do you know that his charater, for purity is good?

A.—I never heard it called in question by any one.

MR. GIBBONS.—My friend stated that I misquoted you, will you now please to state whether you ever heard his character for purity discussed?

A.—No sir, except in this Court Room, just now.

MR. GIBBONS.—So I supposed.

MR. KILGORE.—If I do not mistake, you have known him for about 17 years?

A.—Yes sir.

——

Adam Smith, sworn.

MR. KILGORE.—Do you know the defendant?

A.—I do.

Q.—How long have you known him?

A.—Some five or six years.

Q.—He is your family physician?

A.—He is sir.

Q.—You know other people who know him?

A.—I could not say.

MR. KILGORE.—I ask that question because it is one of the questions which have been stereotyped in this court, and one they confine counsel to, when they examine witnesses as to character.

Q—You say you have known him, do you know other people who know him?

A.—I think the whole community knows him.

Q.—Is he a man very generally known?

A.—I think he is.

Q.—What is his character for purity?

A.—As far as I know him it is good.

Q.—Did you ever hear it called in question by any person who knew him? I do not mean by men prejudiced against him, I mean by those who know him?

A.—No sir.

Cross-Examination.

MR. GIBBONS.—Do you mean you never heard his character for purity called in question?

A.—Not that I remember of.

Q.—You have heard other people question his character for purity have you?

A.—Not that I recollect.

Q.—Did you ever hear anybody speak of his character for purity at all?

A.—I never took any notice of that.

Q.—Whom do you know who know Landis, beside yourself?

A.—I think every body knows him?

Q.—Well name somebody, some of your friends who know him?

A.—I do not anybody except I name half of Philadelphia.

Q.—You cannot name any one individual in the community.

A.—No sir.

Re-direct Examination.

Q.—Do you know Robert Hall?

A.—I do.

Q.—Do you know that he knows him?

A.—I do not.

Q.—Do you know that Adam Smith knows him or Dr. Mincer?

A.—I do not know those gentlemen.

Q.—Well! Do you know a great many men who do know Dr. Landis? Are you acquainted with them in this community although their names do not occur to you?

2

A.—I could not think at present.

A. Hallman, sworn.—

Mr. Kilgore—Do you know Dr. Landis?

A.—Yes sir.

Q.—Do you know other people who know him?

A.—I believe not.

Q.—Don't you know of any persons who know Dr. Landis?

A.—No I believe I do not.

Q.—Do you know Robert Hall, Evans, and Wagner, who have just testified?

A.—No I do not know either one of them.

Q.—Is he your family physician?

A.—I have no family. I have been under his treatment.

Q.—Has he cured you?

Mr. Gibbons.—It makes no difference whether he has or not, you seem to be in good health now.

James Miller, Sworn.

Mr. Kilgore.—Do you know Dr. Landis?

A.—I do sir.

Q.—How long have you known him?

A.—Since 1857.

Q.—You know other people who know him?

A.—Yes sir, I can see a great many people around here who know him.

Q.—What is his general character, by that I mean his reputation, amongst those who know him?

A.—As far as I have heard others speak, they have spoken very well of him.

Q.—Do those who know him best love him most?

A.—That I cannot say.

Objected to.

Q.—Did you ever hear his character for purity called in question by any man or woman who knew him?

A.—I never did.

No Cross Examination.

Gustave Epard, sworn.—

Mr. Kilgore.—Do you know Dr. Landis?

A.—Yes sir.

Q.—How long have you known him?

A—About fourteen years ago, I read a piece in the Public Ledger, and ever since I have heard many of his lectures.

Q.—Are you a member of his congregation?

A.—No sir.

Q.—Do you know others who know him?

A.—Yes sir.

Q.—What is his character for purity amongst those who know him?

A.—For my part I believe he is as pure a man as walks the face of the earth. In 1857, he had a great debate in Jaynes Hall, and I saw hundreds of them there who thought he was the greatest man living.

Q—Have you ever heard his character for purity questioned, by those who knew him or were intimately acquainted with him?

A.—Well I heard a few old women where I lived say they did not like him.

Q.—Did they know him?

A.—I do not know whether they knew him or not, my boarding mistress has said—

Objected to as hearsay, not evidence.

Q.—You never heard those who knew him call in question his character for purity?

A.—No.

No Cross Examination.

H. Bartman, sworn.

Mr. Kilgore.—Do you know the defendant?

A.—I do sir.

Q.—How long have you known him?

A.—About four years.

Q.—Do you know other people who know him?

A.—No sir. I only have an acquaintance myself with him in my official capacity, as a physician.

Q—You know other people who know him.

A.—No sir.

Q.—You have heard these men testify to day, you know some of them?

A.—No sir.

Q.—Do you not know some of them?

A.—No sir.

Q.—Don't you know any person who knows Dr. Landis?

Q.—Have you ever attended his lectures?

A.—One or two times.

Q.—He has been your physician?

A.—Yes sir, I have been under his treatment twice.

Q.—Have you been benefited by his treatment?

MR. GIBBONS.—That is inadmissable, it is not evidence, I do not see why we should waste time in this case.

Q —Did you ever hear his character for purity questioned?

A.—I never heard any direct conversation about his character for purity, never heard it questioned, neither spoken of.

Mrs. Lizzie Hall, sworn.

MR. KILGORE.—Do you know Dr. Landis?

A.—Yes sir.

Q.—How long have you known him?

A.—For seven years.

Q.—You know others who know him?

A.—Yes sir.

Q.—Do you know his character for purity?

A.—I think I never heard anybody call his character for purity in question.

Q.—Has he been your family physician?

A.—Yes sir. That is the way I became acquainted with him.

Q.—How long has he been your family physician?

A.—For seven years.

Q.—He so continues?

A.—Yes sir.

Q.—You consider his character for purity good?

A.—Yes sir.

Cross-Examination.

MR. GIBBONS.—Mrs. Hall, you are the wife of Robert Hall?

A.—Yes sir.

Q.—Did you ever hear Dr. Landis' character for purity, made the subject of discussion?

A.—I have heard that he was so pure that he was considered wicked.

Q.—When did you hear that?

A.—At different times.

Q.—How lately?

A.—I cannot tell how lately.

Q.—Since he was arrested?

A.—No sir.

Q.—You have not heard anybody say anything about it since he was arrested?

A.—No sir. I have seen nobody but his wife since he was arrested.

Q.—You say so pure that he was wicked?

A.—Well that he was mistaken, people mistook him.

Mrs. Mary Snow, sworn

MR. KILGORE.—Do you know Dr. Landis?

A.—Yes sir.

Q.—How long have you known him?

A —Six years.

Q.—Is he your family physician?

A.—Yes sir.

Q.—You know others who know him?

A.—Yes Sir.

Q.—What is his character for purity?

A.—The best that ever was.

Mrs. Cooper, sworn.

MR KILGORE.—Where do you reside?

A.—1016 Stiles St.

Q.—Do you know Dr. Landis?

A.—Yes sir.

Q.—How long do you know him?

A.—Three or four years.

Q.—Is he your family physician?

A.—No sir.

Q.—Do you know others who know him?

A.—Yes sir.

Q.—What is his character for purity?

A.—Well I can only speak of my own opinion.

Q.—Have you ever heard others speak of him?

A.—No sir.

Q.—Did you ever hear his character for purity brought in question?

A.—I never heard it spoken of.

Mrs. Wagner, sworn.

MR. KILGORE.—Where do you reside?

A.—Tenth street.

Q.—What number?

A.—Number 433.

Q.—Do you know Dr. Landis?

A.—Yes sir.

Q.—How long have you known him?

A.—Five years.

Q —Do you know others who know him?

A.—I have very slight acquaintance with other people who know of him.

Q. Have you heard others speak of him frequently?

A.—Yes sir.

Q.—What is his character for purity?

A.—Perfectly good.

Cross-Examination.

Mr. Gibbons.—Did you ever hear it talked of at all?

A.—No sir.

Mr. Bradfield, affirmed.

Mr. Kilgore Do you know Dr. Landis?

A.—Yes sir, I have known him a year and a half.

Q.—Do you know others who know him?

A.—I have met several at his lectures, to whom I talked of his system of treatment, but the question of his moral character was never brought in question before me, I was treated for weak eyes.

F. W. Steiger, sworn.

Mr. Kilgore.—Where do you reside?

A.—Number 26 north 4th street.

Q.—Do you know Dr. Landis?

A.—Yes sir.

Q.—How long have you known him?

A.—Four or five years.

Q.—Do you know others who know him?

A.—Yes sir.

Q.—What is his character for purity?

A.—Very good to the best of my knowledge.

Cross-Examination.

Q.—When did you hear it spoken of.

A.—Never heard it questioned to my knowledge.

Q.—When did you hear it spoken of, his character for purity?

A.—It has been some years ago.

Q —Not lately?

A.—No sir.

R. M. Pancoast, M. D. affirmed.

Mr. Kilgore.—Do you know Dr. Landis?

,A.—I do sir.

Q.—How long have you known him?

A.—Ten or twelve years.

Q.—Do you know others who know him?

A.—I do.

Q.—What is his character for purity?

A.—I do not remember ever hearing anything said against him for purity.

Q.—You never heard it brought in question?

A.—I remember hearing persons say that they had no doubt of his sincerity.

Dr. Rittenhouse affirmed.

Mr. Kilgore—Do you know Dr. Landis?

A.—Yes sir.

Q.—How long have you known him?

A.—About six years.

Q.—Do you know others who know him?

A.—Yes sir.

Q.—What is his character for purity.

A.—Very good so far as I know.

Q.—Did you ever hear it questioned?

A.—Not with regard to his purity, I have heard his doctrines. questioned.

Cross Examined.

Mr. Gibbons.—You never heard his character for purity discussed?

A.—No sir.

Mrs. Sarah Wadlow, sworn.

Mr. Kilgore.—Where do you reside?

A.—533 South Street.

Q.—You are a married woman?

A.—Yes sir.

Q.—You know this defendant, Doctor Landis?

A.—Yes sir.

Q.—Is he your physician?

A.—He is sir.

Q.—You know other people who know him?

A.—Yes sir, I know some persons who know him.

Q.—What is his character for purity?

A.—Well! All I know, that know Dr. Landis, speak well of him.

Q.—Have you attended his private lectures to females?

A.—No sir, I have not attended his private lectures to females.

Q.—Have you read this book, Madam, that is in question?

A.—I read some of it.

Q.—Have you been benefited by it?

A.—Yes sir.

Mrs. Wagner, re-called.

MR. KILGORE.—You are a married woman?

A.—Yes sir.

Q.—Have you read the book in question?

A.—I have sir.

Q.—Have you been benefited by it?

A.—Very much.

Objected to.

Cross-Examination.

MR. GIBBONS.—Will you please to point out what part has benefited you?

A.—The whole of it.

Q.—Will you please point out any particular part that has benefited you?

A.—I do not know any particular part, the whole of it has been to my benefit.

Q.—In what way has it benefited you?

A.—In every way for my health.

Q.—You cannot point out any particular part that has benefited you?

A.—It is all good that is in it.

MR. KILGORE.—So say I.

Francis Parker, sworn.

MR. KILGORE.—Do you know Dr. Landis?

A.—Yes sir, I know him.

Q.—Do you know others who know him?

A.—Yes sir, I know a great many people who know Dr. Landis and I have known him for fifteen years.

Q.—What is his character for purity amongst those who know him?

A.—I know nothing objectionable to his moral character.

Q.—Did you ever hear any person who knew Dr. Landis speak aught against his character for purity?

A.—I never did, I never heard anybody speak anything prejudicial to his character.

Q.—Have you read this book in question?

A.—Yes sir, I have.

Q.—Has it benefited you?

Objected to. Objection overruled.

A.—I just looked at the book, I did not examine it closely. I should call it a medical work. I do not think there is any objection in it.

Q.—Are you a druggist?

A.—I was brought up as a druggist. My father was an English physician. Hence I can see nothing——

MR. GIBBONS.—I object to this.

MR. KILGORE.—The truth is to be suppressed in this case, according to law.

MR. GIBBONS.—The trouble is that you wish to bring in so much truth, that it makes it burdensome.

MR. KILGORE.—The more truth the better.

Mrs. Hall, re-called.

MR. KILGORE.—Have you read this book in question, Mrs. Hall?

A.—Yes sir. I think the advice it contains is calculated to benefit women.

MR. GIBBONS.—No matter what you think.

Cross-Examination.

MR. GIBBONS.—Will you please to point out so much of the advice madam, as has benefited you?

A.—No sir.

Q.—Have you read it all?

A.—Yes sir.

Q.—Will you please to point out what has benefited you, madam?

A.—I do not say it benefited me, I say it contains advice, which would benefit.

Q.—Did I understand you to say that you were benefited by anything contained in this book? In health or in any other way.

A.—Yes sir.

Q—Now, will you point out what benefited you?

A.—I say it contains hygienic advice.

Q.—Igenic, advice?

A.—Yes sir, hygienic advice.

MR. KILGORE.—She said, hygienic advice.

Mr. GIBBONS.—Only she dropped the 'h,' that's all.

Q.—Will you please point out something or other that did benefit you?

A.—Did I understand you correctly.

Q.—I inquire whether I understood you to say, that there was something in that book, you did not know had benefited you, but you thought it might benefit you? Can you point out anything that might benefit you?

Mr. Kilgore.—You must answer his question, Mrs. Hall. Here is where the obscene part comes in, when the District Attorney badgers a witness.

———

John Keihl, sworn.
Mr. Kilgore.—Do you know Dr. Landis?
A.—I do.
Q.—How long have you known him?
A.—Altogether 8 or 10 years.
Q.—Do you know other people who know him?
A.—I have seen him talking to people. I never paid attention. He lived in the same house with me for two years.
Q.—You know other people who know him?
A.—Yes sir.
Q.—Now, with those who know him, not those who slander him, and can't understand him——
Mr. Gibbons.—That is not a proper question, two-thirds of the world might slander him and others speak well of him.
Mr Kilgore.—I hav'nt finished the question.
Q.—What is his character for purity?
A.—I know nothing myself of it?

———

Mrs. Thwait, sworn.
Mr. Kilgore.—Do you khow Dr. Landis?
A.—Yes sir.
Q.—How long have you known him?
A—About six years.
Q.—Has he been your family physician?
A.—He has been my physician.
Q.—Do you know other people who know him?
A.—Yes sir.
Q.—Amongst all those who know him, what is his character for purity?
A.—It is good.
Q.—Have you read this book, and has it benefited you.
A.—Yes sir.

Cross-Examination.

Mr. Gibbons.—Have you children, madam?
A.—I have had. I have buried two.
Q.—You have no children now?
A.—No sir.
Q.—When did you read this book.
A.—About three years ago.
Q.—You read it when it first came out then?
A.—Yes sir, I suppose it was.
Q—Have you a husband, madam?
A.—Yes sir.
Q.—You say you have been benefited by this book?
A.—Yes sir.
Q.—Will you please to point out what part has benefited you?
A.—It has all benefited me, every part of it.
Q—Without any exception?
A.—Yes sir.
Q.—Are you a member of Dr. Landis' church?
A.—Yes sir.
Court.—What kind of a church is it.
Mr. Kilgore.—It is the First Progressive Christian Church, and I think perhaps the most christian of any in Philadelphia. I'm an expert on that.
Court.—Is this book part of the doctrine of the church?
Mr. Kilgore,—No sir the book is founded upon the teachings of Christianity, every word of it, as far as the statements of medical science are concerned.
Court.—Then the book is not taught in the church?
Mr. Kilgore.—The gospel is taught in the church, the Gospel of Christ.

———

Nicholas Beechy, sworn.
Mr. Kilgore.—Have you read this book?
A.—Yes sir.
Q.—Has it benefited you?
Mr. Gibbons.—I think we have gone far enough on this point.
Mr. Kilgore—Will the witness answer the question. He is on the stand. Has it benefited you?
A.—I do know that it did.

Q.—How long have you known Dr. Landis?

A.—About two years.

Q.—Do you know others who know him?

A.—Yes sir.

Q—What is his character for purity?

A.—Good.

Court.—How many witnesses have you called on character now?

Mr. Kilgore.—I do not know your Honor.

I. P. Benner, sworn.

Court.—Is this a witness as to character?

Mr. Kilgore.—He has been a music teacher in this church.

Mr. Gibbons.—I object to any further evidence on this question.

Court.—You said you had some physicians as reserve witnesses, I think you had better call them. The fact which you have offered to prove is established all it can be.

Mr. Kilgore.—Do I understand your Honor that I cannot examine this witness with regard to this book whether it has benefited him?

Court.—There must be an end to this thing and when all has been said on the subject which can be said, I think there is no use in evolving further facts.

Mr. Kilgore.—I now offer the affidavit of Dr. McClintock.

Mr. Gibbons—We object to the contents of the affidavit being read.

Recess of fifteen minutes.

Miss Jennie Hall, sworn.

Mr. Kilgore.—Are you the bookkeeper of this defendant?

A.—I am.

Q.—How long have you been employed in that capacity?

A.—Five years next June.

Q.—Are you the daughter of Robert Hall and Mrs. Hall who have been examined?

A.—Yes sir.

Q—Are you a member of that church?

A.—Yes sir, I am.

Q.—Do you know as to the money accounts of the defendant during the past year, how he has spent his money?

Mr. Gibbons.—We object to this.

Mr. Kilgore.—The gist of this offence, is *malice*, provided the jury come to the conclusion that this book is obscene. If it is not obscene, the Commonwealth's case falls; if it is obscene and the Commonwealth fail to prove *malice*, the Commonwealth's case falls. We bring this witness to show that during the past year, this defendant has expended over $5,000 in this cause for the advancement of these doctrines, in reference to right generation according to the laws of nature and that he did not publish this book for the purpose of making money. I think that bears directly upon the point of intent or motive, and I hope my brethren will not object to it.

Court.—I do not see the gist of it.

Mr. Kilgore.—Will your Honor note an exception.

Q.—You are a member of the 1st Progressive Christian Church?

A.—Yes sir.

Cross-Examination.

Mr. Gibbons.—Is that the church which is advertized in this paper you referred to?

A.—Yes sir, that is the church.

Re-direct Examination.

Mr. Kilgore.—You have been five years the book-keeper of this defendant?

A.—Yes sir.

Q.—Do you know what motive actuated the defendant in the publication and sale of this book?

Mr. Gibbons.—We object to this question as being the one previously overruled.

Mr. Kilgore.—Do you know other people who know him

A.—I do.

Q.—Many?

A.—Yes sir.

Q.—What is his character for virtue, purity, morality, humility and all the Christian graces?

Mr. Gibbons.—We object to the question.

Mr. Kilgore.—What is his character for purity?

A.—The very best that a man could have.

Mr. Kilgore.—That is good enough.

Testimony for the defence here closed.

OPENING ARGUMENT FOR THE COMMONWEALTH

BY

HON CHARLES GIBBONS,

District Attorney.

———•••———

MAY IT PLEASE YOUR HONOR,
GENTLEMEN OF THE JURY

As I stated to you at the commencement of this case, the bill of Indictment which you will have in charge presents the defendant with publishing, selling and delivering to one Breneiser, a certain filthy and obscene book called "The Secrets of Generation." That is the first count. I have shown you a book of that title.

The second count charges him with publishing a certain filthy, infamous and obscene book, entitled "The Secrets of Generation."

These are the two counts, in this indictment upon which you will be called upon to pass. In relation to the first count, I presume, upon the question of the sale of the book, you can have no doubt. Mr. Breneiser, has testified to you, clearly and distinctly that he purchased this book and some other books from the defendant. That fact being clearly established you are then to consider whether this is a lewd and obscene book. As to that question, gentlemen of the jury, I have only to say, that the book must speak for itself. I will point out to you some portions of it, which you can read when you retire to your room. I should be very sorry to read them to this public audience, and I do not believe, gentlemen of the jury, that there are a dozen men in this court room, who could stand up in the face of this audience and read without shame and confusion that portion of the book alluded to, to which I shall hereafter direct your attention.

As to the second count in this indictment, which charges that the defendant has exposed for sale this particular book—there is other evidence than the testimony of Mr. Breneiser. You might find the fact, gentlemen of the Jury, from his testimony, he bought this book, and the defendant had it for sale. But we have his own declaration, the declaration of the defendant, the very strongest evidence upon that point which you can possibly have. This paper, gentlemen of the Jury, which was handed by the defendant to Mr. Breneiser, so far as it refers in any of its columns, to this particular book is a declaration of the defendant himself respecting it.

MR. KILGORE.—Your Honor, I did not understand that that paper was in evidence except the advertisement of this book, though the District Attorney intimates to the jury that there are other allusions to it besides what appear in the advertisement. Of course the jury would have to read the paper all through before they would find out these points, if it is not all in evidence it is improper for him to make that statement.

MR. GIBBONS.—I desire to show, may it please your Honor, the advertisement of the book for sale and I propose to show it by the declaration of the defendant in this paper.

MR. KILGORE.—Your Honor, it is all admitted, there is no need of any proof.

MR. GIBBONS.—I prefer to lay before the jury this declaration, of the defendant—"circulation of the Sharp-Shooter, twenty thousand, with a rapid increase, it goes throughout the Union, editors who receive copies of the Sharp-Shooter and Anti-Fogy, will confer a favor by communicating with their reformatory friends. Those who wish to regularly exchange, will *ex* their papers, when we place them upon our special *ex* list for a year."

Here then is a paper which according to the declaration of the defendant, circulates its twenty thousand copies, and is rapidly increasing, and this paper, contains an advertisement of this book, in these staring capitals which you see before you:

"Read! Dr. Landis." A strictly private "book for married persons, on 'The Secrets "of Generation." This looks, gentlemen of the jury, very much indeed as though it were a strictly private book, not intended for the public to see. On the title page of this book, gentlemen, you will read, that "This book "must not lie about the house, but every male "and female should read it." Not every married man or every married woman, "but every male and female, should read it."

If, gentlemen of the jury, there is nothing obscene or lewd in this book, we may well inquire why it is that he states upon the title page, that it must not lie about the house. A man who publishes a book, which is to do good to all mankind, and to all womankind, and particularly to that portion of womankind who seem to be connected with this Christian Progressive Church—a book, gentlemen of the jury, published for the benefit of humanity, would not be advertised in this way upon its face.

"It must not be left lying about:" if left lying about, perhaps Mr. Breneiser or some other officer of the law might walk in and pick it up and produce it to the officers of the Commonwealth, and it might possibly result in the conviction of the man who published it. This is why the book is not to be left lying about. This man knows, as well as you will know when you take this book to your room to look upon a few of its pages, that this is a lewd, indecent and obscene publication, calculated to deprave the morals of our youth, and do infinite wrong and injury to society. Not content, with these staring capitals, the advertisement goes on. "This is the book you want, strictly private "book for married persons, on "The Secrets "of Generation." Aristotle excelled, by Si-"mon M. Landis, M. D., D. D., a medical "doctor and doctor of divinity!! Where he got his title of D. D., from, gentlemen of the jury, my learned friends upon the other side have not ventured to explain. They have produced a certificate that he is a graduate of some "Eclectic Medical College," here in the City of Philadelphia, which was in existence in the year 1850. "It contains the pith of 24 of his popular private illustrated lectures, on sexual, psychology, etc.," "price one dollar," for sale only by Dr. Landis, at his office, corner of 13th St. and Girard Avenue, Phila., forwarded sealed, prepaid, by return mail, upon receipt of price.

MR. KILGORE.—Dr. Landis sells to both sexes by mail, confidentially. I know you would not read wrong intentionally. You said, "sexual psychology," when it is "sexual physiology." Psychology has reference to the mind, and physiology to the body.

MR. GIBBONS.—I beg your pardon, I must confess my sight is a little imperfect, and my glasses happen to be a little dull, and inasmuch as the defendant is in the psychological school it might not be so far out of the way——

MR. KILGORE.—Physiological.

MR. GIBBONS.—There is some little pschychology in it.

MR. KILGORE.—There is no evidence of that.

MR. GIBBONS.—Being a doctor of divinity, I think he must necessarily deal in psychology. But I correct the mistake it is not printed psychology. Landis sells to both sexes confidentially, gentlemen, nobody but married people must know anything about this book, it is a "Strictly Private Book" advertised in this paper, with a circulation of twenty thousand, and rapidly increasing. Anybody can buy it, gentlemen of the Jury, any son of yours, any daughter of yours, by sending Mr. Landis, or Dr. Landis, as he calls himself, a one dollar note through the post office.

This book has done good to some of the females who have been put upon the stand as witnesses. So they said. But they were ashamed to put their fingers upon that portion of the book which did them good, or explain how the good was accomplished.

Well then we have a series of letters.

Norristown, Pa., Jan. 22. 1866.

Dr. Landis.—I have the honor to present you hereby, the ordered translation of your Secrets of Generation, it is a larger and more difficult work than I had esteemed it at first. There are also different books of this kind in Germany, but I could never find one there which could be put, on the side of this, and it is certain that this written in good German, will excite the very most attention, both in Germany, and among many German people who live in Philadelphia, New York, Baltimore, Washington, etc., who cannot read English. Yours Very Humbly,

ADOLPH KLEIN.

Philadelphia, Jan. 24, 1866.

I will wager "fifty thousand dollars, or ten years wages, of my labor, against ten cents, that my small strictly private book for married persons" on " the Secrets of Generation" containing only thirty-six pages, has more valuable information and advice in it, than any book now in print in the world, of one thousand pages. Who will take the wager, I am in earnest.

S. M. LANDIS,

Cor. 13th & Girard Avenue.

Here we have it again. " The object of Dr. Landis' society is the improvement of the human race." I perceive by the by, that Charles Wagner is the recording secretary. He was one of the witnesses for the defendant, and then here under the list of publications, I find this strictly private book on the secrets of generation. Every body wants it, price one dollar, postage included. *Everybody wants it ! Everybody wants it ! Everybody wants it !* We find here also the advertisement which the lady referred to when testifying of the 1st Progressive Christian Church of Philadelphia. It is the church gentlemen to which these ladies belong.

One column. Strictly private book, that everybody wants " on the secrets of generation." Alongside of it the advertisement of the 1st Progressive Christian Church of Philadelphia.

Now gentlemen of the jury as I said to you in my opening remarks, I do not intend to read what I complain of in this book, but you must read it for yourselves. When you have read it, I think you will have no hesitation or difficulty in saying, that this man is guilty upon both counts of this indictment.

The portions of the book to which I refer, are found on pages 25, 26, 28, 29 and 30. There may be some others, but it is hardly worth while to point them out.

Court adjourned to 10 *A. M., Thursday.*

SECOND DAY'S PROCEEEDINGS.

CLOSINC ARGUMENT FOR THE DEFENCE

BY

DAMON Y. KILGORE, Esq.

MAY IT PLEASE YOUR HONOR,

Gentlemen of the Jury:—The position which I occupy this morning, I would gladly yield to the friend who is my associate in this cause. It is a matter of necessity, that I take the position of Senior Counsel.

This is an important case. It involves more than the good name, the fortune or liberty of any one man, no matter whether he be a physician or a minister. It involves principles.

Never before, gentlemen, did I stand before a jury, in behalf of an individual charged with crime, so impressed with the magnitude of the questions involved in their verdict, as in the present case *with one single exception*. That exception was my first case at the Bar. The defendant was a poor, friendless, kind-hearted young man, charged with the murder of his best earthly friend. I knew very little of the mere forms of law, but in spite of the jeers of my brethren at the Bar, and the contumacious utterances of the officers of this Court (spoken in the presence of the assembled multitude, and in the very ears of my own son,) for eight successive days and nights, without sleep and almost without food, I did all I could do to save that poor man's life. My noble colleague [H. R. Warriner, Esq.] and myself tried in vain to get the truth into that jury box. I was satisfied then, that unless the truth would save George W. Winnemore's life, he could not be saved.

Gentlemen, did I not believe that the truth would free this defendant I would not ask you to acquit him. I love human liberty, but I love the truth more. The technicalities of the practice and forms of law, kept out what was vital to a true understanding of Winnemore's case. The very air was heavy with the mutterings of the multitude, eagerly demanding a victim, and loud was their cry for vengeance. Believing him innocent of the crime charged, we entreated the District Attorney to allow those technicalities to be overruled, for the sake of human life, and to choose the substance rather than the mere forms of law. But the District Attorney was incorrigible; he snuffed the vengeance of the people from afar, (I hope against the feelings of his better nature.) and insisted upon all the forms. He kept out the truth, and our client was convicted and executed. But gentlemen, up to this hour there has never been a word uttered, or a thought expressed in action, to convince either of his counsel that he was not innocent of the crime for which he suffered.

I told William B. Mann, District Attorney at that time, that the sceptre of his power would be taken and placed in other hands.

I hope the present District Attorney will profit by his example. Jurors, in that case, repented of their verdict and gladly prayed a heartless Executive to spare his life.

And now, is there in Philadelphia a man so ignorant, or so blinded by prejudice, that he does not regret that that young man was ever brought to the scaffold. If there is such a man I pity him from my heart of hearts.

One week ago last Sunday night, as SIMON M. LANDIS was about to preach the gospel of truth, in the name of Christ, an officer of the law, armed with a warrant, arrested him, took him to the Central Station and locked him up in a felon's cell.

Doctor Landis, begged for an opportunity to communicate with his family. He asked for a few minutes to go with the officer in order to find bail, but this was denied him. He was compelled, without sufficient clothing, with no fire, to remain till Monday in that cold, damp, filthy cell. *Why was this?* He had been guilty of no crime. Why was he dragged from his pulpit on Sunday night and placed in a loathsome cell? The District Attorney says *he* assumes the responsibility of this prosecution.

Does the District Attorney for the City and County of Philadelphia assume the responsibility of this arrest and what followed? Dare he do it? "Offences will come, but woe unto that man by whom they come. It were better for him that a mill-stone were hanged about his neck and he cast into the depths of the sea than to offend one of these little ones." On a former occasion, Gentlemen, when a certain one had been healing the sick, without drugs, and saying hard things against the popular churches of his time, pronouncing a woe upon them in language quite as severe as any you will find in the "SHARP-SHOOTER," the magistrate was a little doubtful about the propriety of pun-

ishing him to please the popular religious associations of that age, and in the presence of the Priests, Scribes and Pharasees, washed his hands, saying, "*I am innocent of the blood of this just person, see ye to it.*" And all the people cried out " *his blood be on us and our children.*" Look at the terrible results of the responsibility thus assumed. That persecuting people and their descendants have been scattered throughout the earth, oppressed, enslaved, degraded, persecuted by all the peoples of the earth. Verily they have been a by-word and a reproach among the nations. From what I saw of the Commonwealth's witness upon the stand, I presume he is a descendant of this same race of persecuting people. Has he not seen enough of persecution, or have the sufferings of his race failed to purify his blood-thirsty nature from its ancient longing for a victim? In this witness, Gentlemen of the Jury, the only one the Commonwealth could find, I see treasured the vices of seventy generations, accumulated through eighteen centuries. Doctor Landis has been preaching and practising (for he practices what he preaches) in this City for seventeen years. Yet this is the only living witness in the City and County of Philadelphia against this defendant.

This book which will be placed in your hands, as a witness against him, by the Commonwealth, was published in 1866. Why in the name of the man's liberty ; of the purity of public morals and protection of society, if this book is obscene, why did they not commence this prosecution four years ago? Why was it necessary to wait FOUR YEARS, and then arrest this man on *Sunday*, just as he was about entering his pulpit to preach the Gospel? This book was in the hands of thousands of men and women of Philadelphia. If it was obscene, if it was calculated to corrupt the morals of the community, why did'nt they commence this prosecution before? Was it necessary, after they procured the warrant, to put off his arrest two days in order to desecrate the Sabbath—a day set apart for men to attend to the education and development of their religious natures? Ah! Gentlemen, there is something in this case that looks like *religious persecution.* There is something in this case deeper than what appears upon the surface, something back of this prosecution which stamps this whole business with injustice and dishonor. And it is because I have been unable to bring what is behind the curtain forward, that I am so exercised to day.

I could stand here as calm as his Honor, who sits upon the Bench, and although not as beautiful, my face would be as free from anxiety and care as his, were it not for the fact I have been unable to bring before you the whole truth of the case.

I said it looked like persecution. The witness they put upon the stand, the only one the able officers of the Commonwealth could find, in a population of eight hundred thousand, testifies that he went to the office of Doctor Landis at the corner of Girard Avenue and Thirteenth street, and purchased "THE SECRETS OF GENERATION." The Doctor did not consider him a child, he thought him old enough to use properly, this information in regard to God's highest and holiest law on earth—the law of procreation. This man returns to those who sent him, made a complaint against the defendant, upon which a warrant was issued, and instead of arresting this man, who is sapping the very foundation of purity and virtue in this community, if this bill of indictment is true; this Breneiser and his wicked confederates wait until the Sabbath. Nay more, they wait till the daylight disappears and the shades of night come on. A good man, if he has work to do, seeks a proper time in which to do it. Such a man chooses the light of day, while a wicked man prefers darkness because his deeds are evil. This model preserver of purity in Philadelphia, did not choose daylight, when the sun shone beautifully upon the earth, lest the brightness of the sun would be a terrible rebuke to the darkness of his own evil heart.

He waits until Doctor Landis is about to commence his religious services in order to persecute this Christian minister!

Judas, got thirty pieces of silver for betraying Jesus of Nazareth. How much did this Breneiser get for the betrayal of this preacher of the same Gospel, his prototype betrayed and his ancestors crucified. I will not speak of the avarice of this man's ancestors through all the Past; how every prayer of Abraham, Isaac and Jacob was a prayer for wealth; for flocks and herds, for themselves, or for their sons. They never asked for intelligence or justice. They never prayed God to bless their children with virtue or purity, but their prayer was for territory, and flocks and herds to graze upon it. I will not refer you to Shylock who demanded his ducats or his pound of flesh. But, Gentlemen, where, since the time of Judas Iscariot, was there ever a greater exhibition of cupidity and treachery than is seen in the course pursued by this only witness for the Commonwealth.

A minister of Christ betrayed for money! But, I have been told Doctor Landis is an unpopular minister. So was Christ and so were his apostles. So have been the world's redeemers and the world's saviours. Each generation crucifies, through ignorance and prejudice, the men who are their best friends, and who stand up in the face of authority and tyranny to defend their God given and sacred rights.

But time brings ever its retribution. The people see their mistake and mourn in sackcloth and ashes, the cruel act, ignorance and bigotry, caused them to commit. The maligned, persecuted and banished of one generation, become the heroes of the next. Doctor Landis is unpopular with those who have riches acquired by oppressing the poor —who have power in consequence of family, favoritism, wealth or blood. They have not investigated for a lifetime the laws of God, and fearlessly declared them to the masses in order to prevent disease, misery and crime, as has this defendant, and therefore do not understand the laws of Nature as expressed in this little book.

Human nature is the same through all the ages. The same class in the community that crucified Jesus and put his apostles to death; that has persecuted reformers through all time in every nation; that same class of men are crying aloud for the punishment and imprisonment of my client.

Gentlemen of the Jury WHAT IS THE TESTIMONY BEFORE YOU?

Every witness we called, who has known

this man intimately for years, said HIS CHAR-ACTER FOR PURITY WAS GOOD. Some of them said it was the "best in the world." And when one of the witnesses declared that this book, which the District Attorney says is too obscene to put on the records of this Court, had done her good, the District Attorney, forgetting his high position, forgetting that he had the great Commonwealth of Pennsylvania to back him, and therefore he could afford to be generous, aye, forgetting his manhood, undertook to browbeat and badger that witness. He asked this woman of education and refinement, and of as pure and exalted a character as any woman in the District Attorney's acquaintance, *by what part of the book she had been benefited.* She replied "BY ALL PARTS." That woman has been a sufferer by disease, and her spirit has been so purified by suffering, that she can appreciate the teachings of that little book. But I cannot appreciate the forgetfulness of the Commonwealth's officer, or the inexplicable meanness of any man who would undertake to insult or badger such a witness while on the stand. Gentlemen had that Reporter for "THE PRESS" who said that lady gave her testimony without her "h's," followed the teaching of Doctor Landis, his brain would not have been so filled with the fumes of bad whiskey and worse tobacco, as to have penned so mean a slur. If the Commonwealth's officer will find an individual of respectable standing in Philadelphia, whose word is fit to be received in a Court of Justice, who will testify they ever heard from this defendant one impure or obscene word, or who ever knew him to perform an obscene or immoral act, I will abandon this case and join with the District Attorney in asking you to convict. He cannot do it.

The Book-Keeper—Not one of those painted butterflies, who crowd Chestnut street in Grecian Bends and high-heeled boots; their soft hands loaded with diamond rings, whilst their softer heads scoff at God's holy law of maternity; but a young woman of education, who works for her living as all young women should; an honest, industrious, pure-minded, God-loving woman, who would be a prize to the best man in

Philadelphia could he secure her love; that young woman said on the witness stand, there was no man on earth whose character for purity surpassed that of Doctor Landis."

That is the opinion of one who has for five years had charge of the Doctor's Books and who had a good opportunity to learn the real truth respecting this man's character.

If the District Attorney does not object, I will say to you what this defendant's wife told me the day after his arrest. She said to me that although the Doctor was impulsive and sometimes imprudent, and who of us are not? there was no purer man living on this planet than he. There was no kinder or truer husband in the wide wide world, no kinder father than Doctor Landis She knew his character for purity better than any other human being. She understood his motives in writing and publishing this little book. His motives she said were pure and holy.

This is the statement of the defendant's wife. Mrs Landis is one of the most talented and noble women of Philadelphia. I say women, because I love the name. My mother was a woman, and at an early age I followed her dear form to the grave—a grave on the hill side that looks out on Mount Washington and the clear waters of the Saco, that flows at its base, in the Old Granite State. I often think of that mother of her sweet voice of prayer, and of those beautiful lines of Cowper, which I always repeated as I passed by her grave.

"My mother when I learned that thou wast dead,
"Say was't thou conscious of the tears I shed;
"Hovered thy spirit o'er thy sorrowing son,
"Who scarce life's journey had just begun,
"I heard the bell tolled on thy burial day,
"I saw the hearse that bore thee slow away
"And turning from my nursery's window drew
"A long, long sigh and wept a last adieu."

Her spirit still lives, and from her spirit home she encourages me to toil on in behalf of truth. She tells me never to uphold the wrong for all the money clients can bring—but to stand by the right, come poverty or shame. I have never uttered one word to a jury I did not believe, and God helping me, I never will.

This book, they call obscene, was published in 1866. It was published to prevent diseases of women which were caused by ignorance or brutality on the part of their husbands. Doctor Landis had an extensive practice, from which he learned the causes of disease and suffering, and being unable to give to all who needed, the proper instruction in his lectures, he published this book, for the purpose of preventing those diseases and alleviating those sufferings.

The book speaks for itself. If you will turn, Gentlemen of the Jury, to the title page you will find that this is "A STRICTLY PRIVATE BOOK FOR MARRIED PERSONS, on THE SECRETS OF GENERATION." On the same page you find the following—" THIS BOOK MUST NOT LIE ABOUT THE HOUSE, BUT EVERY MALE AND FEMALE SHOULD READ IT."

I assure you Gentlemen there never was a title page placed in any book where the intention was more clearly apparent to have it truly represent the book than this. He put the price at one dollar, for the very purpose of keeping it out of the hands of children.

The District Attorney thought the caution not to let the book lie about the house, was put there because Doctor Landis lacked faith in his book, and when he said "every male and female should read it" it was simply an effort to sell the book. Gentlemen the District Attorney is mistaken. The Doctor meant simply and only this—that the book should not fall into the hands of children, who are unprepared by their years to look into these subjects, as they would be likely to, if it were left carelessly lying about the house.

He meant that every adult person of either sex should read and understand the laws of God as explained in the book.

In the address to the reader, on page 8, the Doctor says—"*The Author does not believe in making 'vain repetitions' or long prayers— when a shorter course answers as well or better.*"

On page 5, he says—" To the honest and " pure-minded individual who labors to love,

"and to be loved ; moreover to be happy, " always endeavoring to make earth heaven- " ly, there can be no subject more interest- " ing and sublime, than the laws of genera- " tion; and in fact everything that is connect- " ed with the origin of human life."

Gentlemen, would to heaven you could view that in the same light I view it, and feel it as I feel it. If there is anything that will reform society, if the race of criminals of Bedford and St. Mary's Streets, who live and fester in their crimes, threatening the liberty and lives of the people in this great city, is to become extinct, it will be through a proper knowledge of and obedience to these laws of God in Generation. Crime begets crime. Tobacco-chewing, whiskey drinking parents can no more generate a healthy and pure-minded son or daughter, than you can make oil and water mix without any chemical change in either.

The sins of the fathers are visited upon the children of the third and fourth generations.

Gentlemen, it is a law of nature that like begets like. Where the parents indulge in lustful passion at the moment of conception the child will have a corresponding organization. You cannot gather grapes of thorns nor figs from thistles.

You cannot have healthy, beautiful, moral, high-minded, parent-loving and God-honoring children, until both parents understand and obey these laws of God in the highest and holiest functions of the organs of generation.

When this is done your criminals will be no more. Your criminal code—now so bad, will not be needed, and such poor wretches as are now eking out a miserable existence in alms-houses, hospitals, prisons and penitentiaries all over the land will be unknown. Houses of prostitution will become extinct, intemperance will cease, and men will walk the earth erect and free, reflecting God's image in the light of day.

These laws of nature apply to animals as well as man. The Patriarch Jacob understood this law when he placed the peeled rods of green poplar, and of the hazel and chestnut-tree, before the flocks that they might conceive before the rods when they came to drink.

He used the rods only with the stronger cattle, and the result was, all the healthy animals were rings-treaked, speckled and spotted, and by his shrewd bargain with Laban, became his property.

They did not allow me to bring in the testimony of men of science upon this most important point. We brought here nineteen educated men, who have made these laws their study—some of whom were practising physicians, others, professors in colleges, in order to prove that the directions given in this book were of the highest importance to mankind;—that they were strictly in accordance with the laws of nature; that the information would tend to bless and elevate rather than to demoralize Society; that the book was neither a libel nor in any way obscene, but Gentlemen, we were not permitted to prove one of these facts.

On page 5 of this book, "SECRETS OF GENERATION," the Doctor says.—

" It is the custom of the human family to " understand how to cultivate the soil for gen- " erating healthful, beautiful, and perfect " grains ; trees; fruits; shrubbery, etc. There " are men who examine the soil, plow, har- " row, manure, and prepare it ; ere the seed " is planted in it ; whilst proper seasons are "chosen for planting that seed, in a scientific " manner, and in the right time of the year. " It is so with the domestic brute creation, " seasons are chosen to generate certain spe- " cies of beings, whilst others of less impor- " tance give no attention to season.

" What a pity, that the generation of hu- " man souls—whose bodies should be made " in God's blessed image—cannot be regarded, " revered, studied, and its laws carefully, ob- " served, especially, since man is of greater " importance than brutes, or plants, and " grains.

" It is written that there is a time and " season for every thing. Yea, and there are " two, and only two, seasons in the year in " which human souls should be generated, if " talented, beautiful, and godly children are " desired.

" There are then, again certain periods in " those seasons which should and must be " observed, if God's image is to be stamped " upon the generations to come ! God knows " if the evil-minded world honor, revere and " obey these natural laws of Jehovah, the " result would be as scientifically useful and " apparent in the young and lovely offspring, " as it is in heeding the laws of agriculture, " horticulture, and the culture of horses, cat- " tle, and the like. But society is so artificial

" and vile that God and nature are considered " vulgar teachers."

" Whenever any thing is generated there " must also be a soil, or something similar to " the earth's soil, wherein the seed must be " planted, and this planting phenomenon must " be performed in a natural manner. Irra- " tional animals, which are not domestica- " ted, are led by instinct. But human beings, " who are educated, not in accordance with " the laws of either common sense, nature, " or an undefiled spiritual monitor ; but who " are erroneously, artificially, and often in- " temperately, gluttonously, and sensually " trained in the schools of the boguisly scien- " tific fashions of an ungodly and ungraceful " people ; therefore, they have no natural in- " tuitive powers whereby to conceive, how " to prepare the soil, in which human souls " are generated, (which soil is woman,) nor " have they wisdom inwrought to complete " the planting phenomenon according to " God's divine Physiological laws."

" Let me again repeat, that no man can im- " prove upon God and Nature. It would be " blasphemy to presume such a thing !"

" Again, after the offspring is once genera- " ted, then comes the most important time to " cultivate the human soil, that the embryo " may grow into a fully developed being, " thereby escaping deformity, idiocy, and nu- " merous other defects, which can be pre- " vented by a full knowledge of the laws of " generation of human bodies and souls; " which, the ignorant, prejudiced and evil- " minded monsters in assumed human shape, " blame upon the Creator who made man ori- " nally, and still wants humanity to be made, " and kept, in His image, that His Son, Jesus " Christ, would be accepted as the Mediator " for, and Redeemer of mankind."

Is that the utterance of a man who publishes *obscene libels* for the sake of corrupting the public morals ?

On page 6, I read as follows :—

" There are, moreover, other points to be " discussed before the "Secrets of Genera- " tion, can be made useful, and before pris- " tine beauty can exist, and love be made the " the ruling and controlling power of the hu- " man family. I refer to courtship, marriage, " and the first sexual intercourse.

" In the first place, *courtship*, at this artifi- " cial and bogus age of fashion and folly, is " looked upon, both by saint and sinner, as a " frivolous and childish transaction, which " should not claim the serious consideration " of the Clergy and Doctors of P..ysic. Both " Church and State have turned this serious " and vital business matter into reckless " merchandise; or entrust it to the perverse " passions of the giddy young, who are inex- " perienced in life's great battle, for them to " follow their impulses of perverted propen- " sities, and negotiate and bargain their entire "beauty, health, and happiness away in a "fit of frenzy, when the priest in saintly "'harness' (as Bishop Alonzo Potter calls it) "pronounces the solemn ordinance and ben- "ediction, 'what God has joined together; "let no man put asunder.' The priest or "clergyman at the same time knowing that "God did not join them together; but it was "unrestrained passion and reckless bargain- "ing, or probably getting married for money "or position; therefore God did not join them "together. but the priest did it for a few dol- "lars. Where God joins two souls together, "there love must be the motive power, for "all true "matches are made in heaven," in "other words, in happiness; and this happi- "ness or heaven can only be attained by "heeding all of Jehovah's laws of life. health, "and His rules of generation and love of off- "spring."

"Marriages are thus made by men and "women of false education and diseased ap- "petite, and confirmed by the traditions of "men; and the true motives and sound laws "of connubial affection, and the enjoyment of "legitimate marriage intercourse are looked "upon as beneath the serious consideration "of men and women of our enlightened "though sinful generation; and the angels "in heaven must weep at the imbecility of "human bodies and souls. All weakness and "failures in life might readily to be avoided, "and true joy attained by every living soul, "if Courtship and Marriage were only per- "formed with the holy and intended motive "of generating beautiful, healthful, and godly "offspring, the generation of which would "promote the pleasures of the true connubial "state a thousand times more than at present, "and the fashionable, useless, and sinful "Womb-Complaints, etc., so prevalent and "ruinous to every natural grace and godly "enjoyment of women would be entirely "unknown; and men would not be dwarfs, "and little-minded tobacco and rum sots, and "playthings for the fashionable and very fas- "tidious ladies to flirt with."

Beginning on page 9, I quote as follows:

"Physiology, common sense, and God, "teach that we being creatures of reason, "should learn all the laws concerned in gen- "erating talented and beautiful offspring, and "rather than make sickly babies make none "at all. No one has a right to generate "more children than the mother can bear in "her womb and nourish at her own breast, "or more than they can afford to raise and "train them up in the way they should go." "But it seems the object of sexual connection "is overlooked and forgotten by saint and "sinner; and instead of holding these organs "most sacred, they make playthings out of "them from the hardness of their hearts and "rottenness of their blood, and from the fact

"that they are slaves to their "propensities, "which are slow to heed the teaching of wis- "dom."

"The man being the head of the family "should always learn what is his duty and "privilege to learn, and obey all the laws of "godly generation to the best advantage. "But the way men are reared and educated, "it seems that every thing else is studied ex- "cept how to be graceful, gentle and wise "in these matters. The man mistakes his "manhood when he thinks woman was "made to gratify his perverted passions, but "when he learns that all the human organs "were make for use, and that over or under "use is injurious and sinful, he will be re- "minded that to know how to use them in "a proper manner, requires *first* a knowl- "edge of their construction and functions."

"It is the man's business to look to his "spouse, that she be healthy before he gene- "rates offspring; but men do not care much "about these things—just so they have plen- "ty to gratify their perverted amorosity—this "is a great sin and shameful outrage upon the "loving and refined sex;—God grant that "men may learn to think and act *like* men "and not worse than brutes!"

"I most earnestly implore the human fam- "ily to give this subject religious and deep "thought, so that our children, grand and "great-grand children, may reap the reward "of our labors and lives!"

Such, Gentlemen of the jury, is the lan- guage of a man, the District Attorney would brand as a corruptor of public morals-a pub- lisher of malicious libel for purposes of gain!

Can you for a moment believe these words were written to demoralize society;—to ex- cite lewd passions and create wicked desires?

Shame burn that man's cheek, who im- pugns the motive of the man who dare de- clare such wholesome truth.

The language may not have been selected with the utmost skill—some words may be objectionable, and perhaps some sentences might better have been left out—but they all combined are unmistakeable evidence of the purity of the author's *motive*, whatever may be said of his choice of words.

Gentlemen—I now come to the question of *obscenity*. The District Attorney has abandoned all parts of this book, except pages 21, 22, 25, and 28.

MR. GIBBONS.—Page 22 is what I partic- ularly called the attention of the Jury to and page 23.

Mr. Kilgore.—What is there on page 23? If I had time I would read the whole book. It is not because I do not endorse its teaching, for I believe every word of it. Every minister ought to preach the same truths at least once every month.

A minister according to Doctor Landis' definition is "*A person who teaches and administers the laws of life and health, and who supplies* REAL *and* ONLY *the real wants of the human body and soul.*" Ministers of the Gospel—should be simply ministers of truth, who follow the example of Jesus in curing diseases of the body and mind, teaching them that the holy (or whole) ghost can not enter into sickly and diseased bodies, for the reason there is so much corruption and impurity that there is not sufficient room for the holy (or whole) spirit to dwell in.

The old Prophets did not think it *obscene* to teach the people in regard to their organs of generation—their functions and how to avoid the evils of misuse. Christ and his Apostles taught the same doctrines as has Doctor Landis in his book. Indeed all through the Bible this subject is treated of according to the enlightenment of that age; and Doctor Landis is only following their example. If there is any one subject upon which the people need light more than upon all others, it is the very subject treated of in this little book under the head "How and when to generate healthy and talented babies!"

Why, gentlemen, look at the one hundred and twenty five murderers in Philadelphia during the last year. I saw ten of them in that dock arraigned at the same hour, together not two months ago!

Look at the thousands of criminals, that crowd your docks, and prisons and penitentiaries, convicted of crimes of lesser grade.

Look at your tens of thousands of drunkards reeling through your streets or daily crowding your station houses—making home, a hell, property and life unsafe, and bringing famine, suffering and misery upon their families! Where does all this woe begin? It begins in generation. The intemperate father stamps his vice upon his child. Criminals are born with natural tendencies to sin. The condition of the parents in the moment of the union of the male and female elements has much to do in shaping the destiny of the new being, for weal or woe through all the future. The part of this chapter complained of as being "too obscene to spread upon the records of this court" gives instruction how to make these conditions such as to give health, beauty and life to the child—to make it reflect God's image, in intelligence and virtue, instead of being filled with disease, and suffering and death. This is obscene says the District Attorney. Why don't he turn his attention to those who make it their business to destroy the life of the new being before it has ever seen the light of day?

Why don't this purity protecting, and society loving witness complain of the abortionists in this city, who get rich by murdering children while yet in their mothers womb? Hundreds of them, with and without Diplomas, live and thrive in Philadelphia to day. The authorities know them, this witness knows them. Why, gentlemen the coroner's Physician told me not long ago the reason abortionists were not prosecuted was because they could not convict them; and the reason they could not get a conviction was, so many of the men in Philadelphia advised and urged their wives to do the same damnable work. Abortion is popular. Fœticide is so common as to go unrebuked, even by the ministers! Gentlemen, Doctor Landis says that "abortions are ruinous"—"never allow a miscarriage to be produced under any pretext, if the mothers life is not endangered." He nobly warns the people of the terrible consequences of this sin. And I tell you every one of these innocents, will live in the spirit world. The union of the two elements male and female, as I before remarked, commenced the life of the new being, generated a human soul, and whether its life is destroyed by Physicians or its parents it will be a swift witness against its murderer in the life to come. No wonder this book is *obscene* to those who uphold these worse than heathen practices. To the pure all things are pure" says the apostle.

How to generate children, so that they

shall be healthy, talented and pure is the *acme* of purity and the most important knowledge that can come to man.

Why, Gentlemen, we sit here from day to day and listen to people, who, having taken a solemn obligation to speak the truth, for a few paltry dollars, or to turn justice aside, deliberately lie. Our public men, with a very few exceptions in order to become rich, or acquire position do not hesitate to do the same thing. Why is lying so common and truth so rare? It is because men are badly born. And after they are born their fathers and mothers teach them that they come from the doctor's saddle bags the turnip patch or carrot bed, instead of teaching them the truth. Parents thus teach their children lies, and they only practice this teaching as they grow older. That is the reason we have so many liars to-day.

COURT.—Part of that may be true. They may come from the carrot field and potato patch first.

MR. KILGORE.—I agree with your Honor. But I see in that remark evidence of scientific acquirement, I did not suppose a man of your great legal attainments ever had time to make.

The District Attorney calls my attention to the last paragraph on page twenty-two:

" These are the true measures for raising " children, and he and she who are not wil- " ling to observe God's unchangeable laws, " had much better have no babies at all; yea, " they should not get married. But, as soci- " ety runs at present, our reformed and " sound physiological doctrines will not be " relished, and therefore will not be put into " practice. Hence, we say, learn how to " prevent generating offspring, which is less ' sinful and more philosophical and Christian " than to bring crippled, puny, miserable. " scrofulous and debauched children into " the world, who are neither loved nor re- " spected by the parents who are so fond of " sexual pleasures; nor who are not lovable, " because God's image is not stamped upon " sickly and half-formed human bodies!"

" Taking, therefore, the evil circumstances " into consideration, we should try and make " the best of life, and hasten to improve the " human race, and abolish all unfavorable " circumstances, and substitute physiological "and Christian conditions."

" The parents have no right to generate "offspring when their circumstances are un- " favorable—therefore let them either ab-

" stain from sexual intercourse, or learn to "*prevent* generating babies until such time " when their circumstances are physiological. " In this manner a *smaller quantity* but *better* " *quality* of children will be born; and those " then born will live to old age, if all things " are equally healthful, and pass gently " through life; loving 'God with all their " hearts, minds, souls, and strength, and their " neighbors as themselves!' and die, finally, " in the natural decay of all things, blessing "and blessed! Oh, what an Eden this Earth " could be made if the people were only " willing to lay aside their prejudices, and " learn and live out all the physical and spi- " ritual laws of our good Creator! Awake, " then, O man! and do your duty to your " wife and children. And wife, be not slow " in appreciating the goodness of true hus- " bands, who are willing to curb their ani- " mal passions for the sake of you and your " child's health and pristine beauty. "

Anything obscene in that? I endorse every word of it. It is obscene only to depraved and diseased minds. No pure man; no pure woman with ordinary intelligence can read that without honoring the man who utters it. I thank you, Doctor, now. In the name of diseased women and sickly children, I thank you for that noble utterance.

What is the next page to which the District Attorney objects?

MR. GIBBONS.—Page twenty-five.

MR. KILGORE.—Now, gentlemen, I have come to the gist of the Commonwealth's case, on page twenty-five. There is nothing on that page or the next that is in the slightest degree obscene to a pure mind.

The ideas expressed are true, and in perfect accordance with natural law. The ideas are better and the language more chaste than are many passages in Byron, Shakespeare, Shelley, and a vast number of medical works, sold to anybody who has the money to pay for them.

If the officers of the Commonwealth, propose to put Doctor Landis in prison for these expressions let them go to your Honor's own library and take out Shakespeare, whose wonderful dramas delight Philadelphia audiences, every night for eight successive weeks, to which the venerable District Attorney has often listened attentively. Then let them extinguish what Mrs. Stowe has left of Byron, who 'touched his harp and nations heard entranced." There is nothing in the "SECRETS OF GENERATION" which can compare with Don Juan.

Yet these are purely literary works not like this book complained of which is purely a medical one. The District Attorney sneered at the Doctor's Diploma, which he received at a regular medical College in this City, and took pains to correct himself when he said "Doctor" by calling him "Mr. Landis."

Mr. GIBBONS.—I beg pardon for dropping the Doctor's title.

Mr. KILGORE.—I forgive you, brother, I thought it intentional but I never strike a man who is down. Titles amount to very little, but we should give every man his due. We could show another diploma Doctor Landis received, as evidence of high attainments in the Medical profession. His book therefore, is a medical book—written by a medical man upon a physiological subject.

Now, Gentlemen, I presume the only word on page twenty-five which can be objected to is the word "heating." Had the Doctor used the word "exciting," they would not have dared to say one one word against it, for we have a stack of books here in which we will show these gentlemen the same thoughts expressed by the word exciting. Doctor Landis uses the word heating in speaking of man, precisely as it is used when applied to animals. Man is an animal. Heating is an Anglo-Saxon word while exciting is derived from the Latin.

Doctor Landis used plain Saxon words, which, though not as euphonious as the Greek, nor as symetrical as the Latin, are more vigorous and powerful than both, and which go directly to the soul of things. Di-coveries in Science within the last eighteen months show that heat is the cause of all motion, whether it be the circulation of the sap in plants or crystalization in minerals. It is the basic principle in that law by which the planets move, and suns and systems revolve in space. It is the most scientific word to use in reference to that divine act in which all the muscles, brain and nervous fluids join to generate a human soul. A soul, Gentlemen, destined to devolope through future years on earth till emancipated from its dusty elements it is free to travel through all the starry realms in God's illimitable kingdom. And yet they object to this word and call it obscene! Gentlemen, Doctor Landis knew that mankind were being destroyed through ignorance of natural laws. On the next page in this book, you will find he gives instruction, respecting the conditions necessary to the proper generation of an immortal soul.

Why, Gentlemen, only yesterday a minister came into my office and related to me a case where a young and beautiful wife was ruined by the husband, through his ignorance of the proper *conditions* for the proper consummation of marriage.

It would be improper for me, to even tell you what we were prepared to prove by those physicians, whose testimony the Commonwealth did not dare to have you hear. You would be astonished, Gentlemen at the number of pale, sickly, nervous and suffering women, who have been made such by their passionate husbands, ignorant of the very laws they constantly violate.

Nay, more; not only are myriads of women rendered wretched by this cause, but diseased and puny children are generated—whose lives are full of misery.

Doctor Landis has had an extensive practice, from which he decided that the greatest good he could do for humanity, was to give them an understanding of these laws of God. The truth is not obscene. Nature's laws are not obscene and the man who understands and teaches them, is a benefactor to mankind. The *Secrets of Generation* should be understood by every parent, and those about to resume the responsibility of parentage. We have proved to you that Dr. Landis did not allow this book to be sold by agents—but that it was sold only in his own office to persons of mature age. If the Commonwealth will produce a single instance of its being sold to any child of either sex, unless that child came with an order from the parent, I will abandon this cause.

As the Commonwealth did not allow us to prove by medical gentlemen that this book is not obscene, we can only compare this work with others against which no charge of obscenity is brought. The public sense of morality and propriety on this subject must decide the question whether this book is obscene.

I hold in my hand a medical work which was bought at public auction in this city, filled with illustrations of the genital organs of both sexes. Why does not the District Attorney prosecute those who sell works of this kind in which the *use* of these organs is fully illustrated by plates? No one will deny that "THE SECRETS OF GENERATION" is harmless in the hands of children compared with illustrations like these. Yet these are medical works, and as such are protected by law. I do not object to these books because they acquaint human beings with their own organism, and thus qualify them to take care of and use properly all the members of the body. In the dark ages, when a few priests monopolized all human knowledge, worked pretended miracles and in consequence of the general ignorance of natural laws, imposed upon the credulity of the people, this information would have been suppressed. But to day, knowledge is the birthright of all the people, and whatever tends to elevate and bless humanity, they have a right to know. A knowledge of the proper use of the organs of generation does this, and therefore should be within their reach.

More than twenty years ago I struggled long and hard to get the Legislature of Massachusetts to adopt Physiology as one of the text books in the Public Schools of that state. The only argument urged against it was that it would be improper or obscene to teach Physiology to children in the schools.

But, Gentlemen, to day not only is Physiology taught in the schools of all grades in Massachusetts and New England, but it is taught in all the advanced schools of the Union.

Gentlemen, less than two centuries ago Massachusetts persecuted Quakers on account of their religion, and executed sensitive persons, accused of being witches.

And I remember, if your Honor please, how the Judge who had presided at these trials afterwards stood up in the church and implored the prayers of the congregation "that the errors he had committed might not be visited by the judgements of an avenging God, on his country, his family or himself." And years later when he came down to his grave, in his diary was found, on the margin of the record of these trials, vae, vae, vae, meaning woe! woe! woe!

Greatly to my surprise, the District Attorney, has gone back almost to that Quaker persecuting, witch hanging Massachusetts, not the Massachusetts of to day which we all revere and love, to the Seventeenth Report for the exact language of this Bill of Indictment.

I call the attention of the Jury to the fact that he did not dare to bring an indictment against Doctor Landis, in the language of modern reports. You had better not have done that my brother. After having searched through the criminal proceedure of Europe and of this country in vain, to find language, for the indictment against this defendant, you had better have abandoned the case and followed the higher and nobler impulse of that great manly heart.

There may be one other word, on page twenty six, to which the District Attorney objects. Doctor Landis has used the word "conductor" instead of the Latin word generally used in other medical works. He is an original man, and has used a word which signifies the natural use of the organ itself. He gives information on this page that many husbands need. Young men about to be married, if they are as pure and virtuous as they desire their wives to be, need this information. No pure minded man or woman, who desires to obey God's laws, as written in their own being, can be demoralized or injured by the instruction given. We have here physicians who have made these laws of Physiology and Hygiene the study of their lives, but the Commonwealth will not allow them to give their testimony that this book is not obscene. As many of these physicians are now listening to my voice. I challenge the District Attorney to allow one of them to testify as to the obscenity of this book. *He dare not do it.* Consequently, you are to judge, without any proof from medical men, whether this medical book is obscene. If the District Attorney will prove to you that this is not a scientific, medical work, that its teachings are not true, in every particular, both in matter and manner, I will abandon the case.

You must remember, Gentlemen, that this book is a strictly private book for married persons. What might be very improper to put into the hands of children, would be very appropriate for married persons.

With this in mind, you are to test this book by the general sentiment of the community, and age in which you live, in reference to obscenity in publications.

In three Philadelphia Sunday papers of this week, I find medicines advertized for the purpose of producing abortion, yet these papers go into the family circle, children read them.

COURT.—If you show twenty improper publications it will be no excuse in this case.

MR. KILGORE—No doubt, your Honor, that is correct. But the question is whether this book of Doctor Landis is obscene. As we have not been allowed to prove by experts that it is not an obscene book, I propose to take the only course left me, namely, to show that the public sentiment of this age not only tolerates medical works much more objectionable than this, but that society tolerates many purely literary publications much worse than anything contained in the SECRETS OF GENERATION.

If I show books in every library, every school, every church, and every family, nay, in the hands of every child, that contain matter more objectionable than anything in this book; that the sentiment of this age, not the dark ages of the past, or the time of the Seventeenth Massachusetts Report, allows the free circulation of books more calculated to arouse the animal passions, and create lewd thoughts, than anything this book contains, then it will be the duty of this jury to say, that this book is not a libel, or obscene under the statute.

There is a book, gentlemen, which the law calls obscene; I sent and purchased it since this case was commenced. It was bought at a bookstore on one of the principal streets of Philadelphia, in an aristocratic part of the city, next door to a church, not far from your Honor's home. That book, filled with obscene plates, is a base libel, a miserable, obscene publication which I call upon the District Attorney to suppress. I am told there are more than twenty places in this city, where such books are sold, four of them on Chestnut street. This book was written, not to benefit mankind, but to inflame the passions. It is written and illustrated in the most amorous and lustful style possible, for purposes of gain.

It is sold, not to married persons only, but indiscriminately to young men and boys, whose diseased and morbid natures crave such loathesome filth. I hope the District Attorney will pay strict attention to those who publish and sell such vile trash, instead of arresting ministers of the gospel, who preach truth for humanity's sake without money and without price.

And here, gentlemen, I am reminded of a question the District Attorney asked one of our witnesses which particularly shocked me. It the hardest thing for me to forget, the un kindest cut of all. He asked her if the church of which Dr. Landis is pastor, was not a " Free Love church. "

MR. GIBBONS —I asked that of a man.

MR. KILGORE.—Well, it was not quite so bad as I supposed. He asked him if his church was not a Free Love church. I will answer him. If it is a Christian Church it is a FREE LOVE CHURCH. Its members love the truth ; love each other and all mankind, even their own personal enemies. They love their neighbors as themselves, and the highest evidence of its being a Christian Church would be in their loving freely, everybody, good, bad or indifferent, wherever man lives throughout God's heritage. Love cannot be too free. Why, Gentlemen, love is the strongest word in the Greek language ; it is the strongest word in the Anglo-Saxon ; it is the strongest word in the English language, come from whatsoever source it may.

Love will go beyond the prison or gallows; it will follow the disobedient son to the lowest depths of degradation and vice, it will go with him to the scaffold and beyond the tomb. It will brave a corrupt public sentiment, which to some sensitive souls, is more terrible than the gibbet or the rack. GOD IS LOVE, and *he that dwelleth in God dwelleth in love and that continually.* The District Attorney did not mean love at all. He meant to ask if his was not a *free lust* church. If you want to find free lust, do not go to a poor, reformatory church, sustained principally by the minister giving nearly all his earnings for that purpose. Such churches have to sacrifice enough from persecution; being called fanatics, crazy and their pastors obscene and libelous, without sacrificing themselves to lust.

No, rather go to your rich, aristocratic churches, whose ministers travel in Europe at the expense of jealous husbands, if you would find free lust.

COURT.—There are a great many things in this argument which are extremely collateral. I think it is better to confine yourself to the subject.

MR. KILGORE.—The District Attorney asked for information and I was bound to give it to him.

COURT.—That can be given to him in private.

MR. KILGORE.—I think it best to give him the information here, if your Honor please. No, Gentlemen I know of no churches struggling in poverty, no true reformers, who believe in free lust. I know of no reformer whether man or woman who does not believe in true marriage, not in law only, but the marriage of one man to one woman so long as they both shall live—a union of hearts which makes a heaven. Doctor Landis believes and teaches this to his church and congregation.

Pardon this digression. I was saying, Gentlemen, that public sentiment tolerated even in literary works, much more objectionable passages than can be found in the SECRETS OF GENERATION.

I might call your attention to Shakspeare's Works, found in every library and in the hands of almost every child. In Venus and Adonis there are passages, calculated to excite lewd passions in both young and old, too obscene to quote, but accessible to every school boy in the land.

Yet Shakspeare was neither a physician nor a minister—he did not write his dramas or sonnets for the purpose of teaching mankind how to obey the divinest functions of their earthly lives. I might refer you to Byron's Don Juan and the bewitching lines of Thomas Moore.

Yet, Gentlemen, this is the literature tolerated in respectable and cultivated socie y to day. These are not medical works giving instruction of the highest importance, in language calculated to make men feel the holiness and purity of true sexual relations.

If the District Attorney succeeds in convicting this defendant, let him prosecute all publishers of the works to which I have referred. Nay more, let him put the Bible out of Society because there are words in it which he must call obscene. You can make no distinction. The motive of Doctor Landis was to give good instruction to his fellow men and I have no doubt the writers of the Bible meant also to do good.

In the Bible you have the account of the two daughters of Lot, getting their father drunk, in order to "lie with him" as recorded in the XIXth chapter of Genesis. I might refer you to the XXIXth chapter of the Book of Genesis; and also the XIXth chapter of Judges 22—29th verses inclusive. I submit, this language is not more refined or chaste than anything you can find in the book complained of. Take the account of Amnon's violation of his sister Tamah, recorded in 2d Samuel XIIIth chapter; and the 27th verse of the VIIIth chapter of the Second Book of Kings. Nothing in Doctor Landis' book will equal the phraseology of many portions of the Bible, which is religiously placed in the hands of every Protestant child in the land. If you convict this defendant, I trust you will prosecute the Bible Society for violating this Statute.

Gentlemen, as farther evidence of public sentiment on this question of obscenity, I might call your attention to scores of books and newspapers sold everywhere in this

40

community, whose influence is far from elevating. Why Gentlemen look to your places of amusement. Such plays as the Black Crook, White Fawn, Formosa and the Can Can crowded your theatres for weeks together. I am told there are public exhibitions much more objectionable than these, not only permitted, but which draw large audiences in Philadelphia.

Yet this humble minister of the Gospel, who dares to follow in the track of the old Prophets, in denouncing the sins, of the people; a man of pure life, is charged with demoralizing society, because he tells the people how to obey the laws of their own being. No wonder there are strong prejudices against this man, whose daily life is a rebuke to the false and fashionable around him. Prejudice banished Aristides, the Just. It gave the hemlock to Socrates, accused of corrupting the morals of Athens, and of making innovations in the religion of his country, although he directed all his energies to the reformation of the morals of the people. Religious prejudices crucified Jesus and sent his followers wandering "in sheep-skins and goat-skins; in caves and dens of the earth;" to be hunted throughout Judea, Mesopotamia and all the countries of the East, and at length brought them to the amphitheatre at Rome to be slain by wild beasts, for the amusement of a corrupt, wicked and Pagan people. The men who labor for the good of mankind will always have enemies. Dr. Landis is an earnest, impulsive, but honest and courageous man, who speaks "right out," as Shakspeare says, "the things that he doth know."

Instead of using Latin terms, he speaks plain English. Shall we complain of a man for teaching the people truths, in language which they can understand, while we permit others to teach the same ideas in a foreign tongue? That the information given in this book is necessary, is not denied.

Not long ago, the daughter of one of the first men in Vermont, died in the Insane Asylum at Brattleboro' because her mother neglected to teach her of the change her system would undergo, at the age of puberty. And when at an evening party, she experienced that change for the first time, she took

counsel of an ignorant servant girl, put her feet in cold water, and went to bed. The result I have told you. A large proportion of the cases of insanity, come from the abuse of the sexual organs.

The people need intelligence on these subjects. Why, Gentlemen, from a work published in 1867, written by a woman. I quote as follows:—"*The evils of sexual abuse lurk in almost every household; they have cursed all the past of humanity, and must curse generations yet unborn. In wedlock the abnormal use of the sexual function is called virtuous, because the law sanctions whatever is done under the cover of marital law; but all the civil laws in the land can never prevent its evil effects. It has produced a race of men, physically weak, but with such strong sexual propensities, that they must be indulged, at whatever cost to wife or children, and at the cost of maintaining a class of outcast females for their accommodation.*"

She says—"Nature will not be cheated, "Beware how you keep your accounts with "her. She will demand of you, 'an eye for "an eye and a tooth for a tooth,' and "future generations shall pay to the utter-"most farthing," for all our abuses of life "as we are paying to-day for the abuses of "the past. 'The sins of the parents shall be "visited upon the children.'' If children were "rightly generated their natural instincts and "intuitions would be correct guides for them "in all the relations of life. No man can un-"derstand or realize the full force and impor-"tance of this truth like mothers who have "been thoughtful enough to trace effects in "their children to ante-natal causes. Children "inherit weakness, sickness and premature "graves; others are cursed with life-long "misery, all produced by the wrong *condition* "of the parents, when neither of them are at "all sensible of the misery they are propagat-"ing. The sensitive nerves of woman should "be in proper *condition* when the child is gen "erated. On page 309, she says: "Mothers "procure abortions and commit fœticide be-"cause the maternal law is so constantly vi-"olated." I know a woman, a church mem-"ber, who procured thirteen abortions in the "space of fifteen years, and at last fell a vic-"tim to her sin. During these fifteen years.

'her whole life was a slowmurder, a suicide.
'And the husband, a church member, too,
'' was he less guilty than his wife? Nay, he
" was in every respect her accomplice. They
" sinned ignorantly, perhaps; nevertheless,
" they could not escape its penalty."

COURT.—It was not ignorance, it was wickedness, malignant wickedness. Nobody can be ignorant as that without they are insane.

MR. KILGORE.—I think they can, your Honor. I think they can sin ignorantly, not knowing the consequences, and that they sometimes do it with a feeling of duty. But I agree with your Honor, it is very wicked, and only shows the necessity of the information given by my client.

The writer of these extracts says further:
" If I speak plainly upon these subjects, my
'' motive must be my apology."

COURT.—What book do you read from, Mr. Kilgore?

MR. KILGORE.—From SEXOLOGY, as the PHILOSOPHY OF LIFE, IMPLYING SOCIAL ORGANIZATION AND GOVERNMENT. By MRS. ELIZABETH OSGOOD GOODRICH WILLARD. Published by J. R. Walsh, Chicago.

Gentlemen, these extracts all go to show that the condition of the mother at the time of conception, stamps weal or woe upon the future immortal being. They all go to prove that the great majority of diseases of women come from these discordant sexual relations, and that intelligence is the only remedy.

Ignorance here, results in intemperance, insanity and crime. Doctor Landis teaches the necessity of preparing the soil, before the seed is sown. He teaches the importance of right conditions, in the moment of generation, in order to stamp God's image upon the newborn soul. I have spoken to you of the numerous professional murderers of unborn children, in this city, who defy the law. The crime of abortion or fœticide could nowhere exist, were not conditions of maternity forced upon woman against her will? Doctor Landis gives information that strikes at the very root of these evils, and if practised, would to use his own choice words, " enable a holier element to rule the family *circle and aid in making earth a paradise.*"

Until recently, many of the truths given in this book were unknown. Within a few years the microscope has revolutionized medical science, and good physicians of all schools feel more than ever the necessity of giving light to the people upon these subjects. Maternity is the end and aim of sexual union. Holy, divine, it is worthy the attention of our best minds, for this primary condition of life, determines the future of every human soul.

Gentlemen, I now come to the LAW. This bill of indictment charges the defendant with publishing and selling a *certain lewd, wicked, scandalous, infamous, filty and obscene printed book entitled* SECRETS OF GENERATION. I agree with the District Attorney in his definition of a libel. " It must be a malicious publication, tending to injure society at large to defame the memory of the dead or destroy the reputation of the living." Under act of Assembly of March 31, 1860, "*if any person shall publish or sell any filthy and obscene libel, &c.,* and "*shall be convicted thereof, such person shall be sentenced to pay a fine not exceeding five hundred dollars, and undergo an imprisonment not exceeding one year.*"

To justify a conviction of this defendant under the law, it is necessary to prove three things: 1. *That the defendant published or sold the book described in the indictment.* 2. *That the book is obscene,* and 3. *That it was published through malice.* That Dr. Landis published the book is admitted. That the book is obscene for the uses and purposes for which it was published, we deny. On this point the Commonwealth have not offered any testimony except the book itself. As we were not allowed to prove the real character of the book by medical experts, we have shown you what is public sentiment in regard to obscenity. They have not produced a particle of testimony to prove malice.

Now, gentlemen, under the statute I think this case is not made out. I shall ask his Honor to instruct you that " the law will not presume a communication to have been made through malice, which was made confidentially in good faith and in discharge of a legal, social, or moral obligation, and through benevolence to the public."

The Secrets of Generation is a communication "made confidentially;" it is "a strictly private book for married persons," as is seen on its title page. It was sold only at the office of Dr. Landis, to adult persons, as one of the witnesses testified.

Mr. Gibbons.—Who swore to that?

Mr. Kilgore—If you have any doubts about it I will call the witness. If you should find, gentlemen, the book to be, in your opinion, *obscene* for the uses and purposes for which it was intended, which we deny, even then you could not convict, unless it was published with a bad intent. There is nothing in the book calculated to inflame the passions or excite lewd feelings, but on the other hand, the author appeals to God; to the human conscience; to the higher and holier nature in all he says.

He wrote this book in discharge of a "*social and moral obligation, and through benevolence to the public.*" This defendant is a physician; he has a professional relation to the public, and is under obligation to promote their physical well-being. He is also a minister; a watchman upon the walls of Zion, and, however derelict in their duty others may be in regard to these social evils, knowing their cause and cure, he feels it his duty to speak out. He obeys the command to "cry aloud and spare not;" "to show the people their transgressions, and the house of Jacob their sins."

He has a public duty in two capacities; he has to do with the physical interests of the people as to their bodies, and the spiritual interests of the people as to their souls—a double obligation to give them instructions, necessary for their temporal and spiritual salvation. Christ healed the bodies as well as the souls of men. He commissioned his followers to do the same thing. This defendant believes in Christ. He strives to reach his doctrines and to imitate his example. The District Attorney will strive to make you believe this book was published for the purpose of making money. We were prepared to show how he made money and how he used it. No, the inspiring motive which influenced Dr. Landis in the publication of the Secrets of Generation was "benevolence to the public."

The law says: "If the production was honestly meant to inform the public mind and warn them against supposed dangers in society—though the subject may have been treated erroneously—then, however the judgment of the jury may incline them to think individually, they should acquit the defendant. If the jury doubt of the criminal intention then also the law pronounces that he should be acquitted."

That the information was honestly meant to inform the public and warn people of the danger of violating the laws of nature in sexual relations cannot be doubted. If the subject is treated erroneously—if the words are not well chosen—the sentences ungrammatical, as some of them are, or if the conclusions to which the author arrives are false—even then you should acquit. This is the law of libel in England and in the United States. If the jury doubt of the criminal intention, it is their duty to acquit. They should do this, however objectionable the book might be, if the *intention* was good. Such is the law of libel in Pennsylvania and by it our courts and juries and district attorneys are bound.

Again, his Honor will doubtless instruct you that "a communication made bona fide "upon a subject matter in reference to which "he has a duty, is privileged, if made to a person having a corresponding duty, although it contained criminating matter, which without this privilege would be slanderous and actionable." I have copied these points from the decisions of Lord Mansfield, Chief Justice Marshall, and others of more recent date.

Dr. Landis, made this communication upon a subject matter in reference to which he had a solemn duty. As a physician and clergyman, it was his duty to promote the health of the people, as well as to warn them of the dangers of sinning against the divine law of generation.

His duty was all the more imperative, as he had given his whole life to acquisition of knowledge upon these subjects. He had made it a specialty. He lectured every night in the week till his voice became hoarse, in enlightening the people of both sexes, eager to know the truth. He was constantly receiving letters from persons at a distance, inquiring what they should do to be saved —saved from suffering, disease and death. By advice of friends he published THE SE- CRETS OF GENERATION, to benefit those pa- tients he could not treat personally.

We could show you a stack of letters from all parts of the country, many of them writ- ten by men and women of high standing, expressive of their thanks for the benefit they have derived from this book. The Dr. has received letters from France and Germany, asking the privilege of translating it into the language of those countries. Ah! gentlemen future generations will do him justice. Gal- lileo told the people the world moved and they punished him. In a moment of weak- ness he recanted, but immediately mindful of the truth of his position, he said " but it does move nevertheless. " Yes, gentlemen, the world does move. Every revolution of this little planet, brings us into new relations and new conditions. Scientists are busy studying these relations to other planets and their results. So each day of our human life brings us into new relations with all the past and shapes the future.

Harvey, while investigating the secrets of generation, discovered the circulation of the blood. He met with the fate of all advanced minds—he was unpopular, and lost his practice. But who can tell the influence of that discovery upon the world to-day. The endosmose and exosmose process in the minute cells of the lungs, is not more sure to change the human body, than that the truths in this book will outlive the prejudices and institutions of to-day and mould the coming man. My client had a duty to mankind ; as soon as he discovered the truth to declare it in the most efficient mode to the people, He felt his responsibility as a physician to proclaim the truths he discovered.

The learned Court will doubtless instruct you that according to the present law of libel " it is the undoubted right of every member " of the community to publish his own opin- " ions on all subjects of public and common " interest, and so long as he exercises this in- " estimable privilege candidly, honestly and " sincerely with a view to benefit society he " is not amenable as a criminal. But where " public mischief is the object of the act and " the means used are calculated to effect that " object, the publication is noxious and inju- " rious to society, and is therefore criminal. "

Applying this law to this case, you would be bound to acquit this defendant.

Again : " If the jury find the teaching of ' this book calculated to benefit the persons " to whom it is dedicated—they should ac- " quit the defendant. "

We have proven to you by one or two witnesses that the teaching of this book had benefitted them. The Commonwealth would not allow us to prove that this book was cal- culated to benefit all the persons for whom it was written. They have not been able to find one solitary individual who has ever been injured by it, and as it has benefitted two, we may conclude it would benefit oth- ers. I have requested his Honor to charge you that " if the jury believe the defendant ' have in view the benefit of society—how- ' ever wrong the ideas, or objectionable the " language—there is no malice and he should " be acquitted. "

The law will not presume malice in this case and as the commonwealth has failed to prove it, it is your duty to acquit. Prejudice must not come in. If you find any prejudice in your minds against this defendant, I ask you, as you hope for happiness, to rise above it.

The law and the testimony constitute the standard to which we must bring this case.

The *motive* for publishing this book, speaks for itself. Every page of it appeals to the moral nature, in the most solemn and impressive manner, and teaches hu- manity how to be obedient to the higher laws of God.

Pardon me Gentlemen for detaining you so long. It is because this trial has to do with the future of society; with principles higher than you and me and this Honorable Court, that I have been thus lengthy. The District Attorney is to follow me. I do not underrate him. You know his great abilities. He is great in law, great in elo- quence, great in experience and greater still in his power to control the minds of other men. He is very dignified. I know him to be a high minded gentleman, of strong prejudices and able to make the worse appear the better reason. Treat him kindly; listen to his eloquence, but do not allow yourselves to be influenced against your better judgement by one word that falls from his authoritative lips.

You are about to decide the guilt or innocence of this defendant. You are to say whether he is an enemy, who attempts to degrade and demoralize mankind, or whether he feels earnestly and deeply the wrongs in Society and strives to use his influence to have those wrongs righted.

You are to decide whether that noble wife, who feels as no other being in this Court House can feel for her husband, with all the impulses and affections of her woman's heart, is to be disgraced by the conviction of the man she loves.

You are to decide whether those beautiful children—two of whom were born at the same hour, not five months ago—living witnesses of the purity of their father's character and life, are to be dishonored by your verdict.

Gentlemen—however others may judge, I pray you to remember that this book only teaches the highest laws of our being—that it is *true* and *natural*, and that to a pure mind THERE IS NOTHING NATURAL, OBSCENE.

CLOSING ARGUMENT FOR THE COMMONWEALTH

BY

Hon. Charles Gibbons, District Attorney.

GENTLEMEN OF THE JURY:

You have listened with great interest to the very long, and very able address of my learned and eloquent friend, but if it had a little more to do with the question which you are to decide perhaps I should have more to say about it than I probably shall have, in the few remarks, which I propose to submit to you in this case.

I have no doubt of the sincerity of my learned friend, I have no doubt of his love of mankind, or of his love of womankind. I believe Gentlemen of the Jury, that he would go forth this day in defense of woman as valiantly as that famous Knight Errant of Spain, who levelled his lance with equal courage against, wind-mills and flocks of sheep, and mailed Knights, but gentlemen of the jury, my learned friend, said some things, in relation to this case that I was sorry to hear, remembering the fact that he himself once stood at the desk of the minister of the gospel.

Remembering the fact, gentlemen that he was once a vice gerent of this Saviour whose name he so often invoked; in the course of his speech here.

I was sorry to hear him say that he would not hesitate to read to his own children every word, that is contained in this book and that he would not hesitate if he now were a preacher to promulgate it in the congregation and from the pulpit which he occupied.

MR. KILGORE.—Mr. Gibbons I said to promulgate the same truths. I might perhaps have some change in the wording but the same principles there expressed, I would proclaim.

MR. GIBBONS—I am glad to hear the explanation, gentlemen, because it implies, that his client has been guilty of an obscenity in the publication of this book that he would under no such circumstances be guilty of.

MR. KILGORE.—Not at all.

MR. GIBBONS.—Now gentlemen, you and I have no business, to entertain any feeling about this case, we are simply here in the performance of a high public duty.

Simply to vindicate and sustain the majesty of the laws under which we live.

Simply to protect, that most sacred place, that any of us may claim as our home or home circle, and the family fireside, from the invasion of lewd and obscene publications of the man now on trial.

That is your duty and it is mine. It is nothing to the point gentlemen, that this book is obscene, or that book is obscene. That there are medical works circulating among medical men, that contain obscene pictures, and obscene desciptions of the human anatomy.

It is nothing gentlemen, of the jury that my learned friend can send and purchase disgusting book at a book store in the city of Philadelphia, all this has nothing on the face of the earth to do with a case like this. Because, Gentlemen of the Jury, one man publishes an obscene book and violates the law, you will agree with me in saying that that does not justify another in doing the same thing.

If one of those poor men now sitting in the dock, waiting their trial, perhaps for some felony, should be found guilty of that felony, why Gentlemen of the Jury, that does not justify you or me or any man, in committing a felony, or even if he were to go unpunished or unwhipped of justice, that would not justify us in perpetrating the same crime. No, Gentleman there are no precedents that can justify crime under any circumstances, there is no precedent that can justify an open and flagrant violation of the laws of the land, under which we live. There is nothing that can justify this man who stands before you, producing his diploma as a medical doctor, in assuming to himself the title of Doctor of Divinity and wearing the livery of Heaven for the purpose of serving the purposes of the Devil.

MR. KILGORE.—Will you allow me to correct you there, I never thought of that until you mentioned it. I can show you how that title belongs to him.

MR. GIBBONS.—God forgive the man who ordained him, that is all I have to say to that. I do not mean to refer very much, gentlemen, to the personal remarks of my learned friend, as applicable to myself. Many of them highly complimentary, more complimentary, I am sure, than I deserve, and many of them rather of an opposite character. I do not know, gentlemen, which will weigh the most in the scales of justice, if any of them shall weigh anything at all.

But my learned friend found fault with a question which I put to one of his witnesses, a question, gentlemen, that was strictly upon cross examination, viz: "Whether the church to which he belonged was a Free-Love Church." You remember, gentlemen, that my learned friend introduced that witness upon the stand, a man and not a lady, inquiring whether he was a member of a particular church. He said "Yes," he was a member of a church, "that is advertised in this paper, called the First Progressive Church of Philadelphia. And then I asked upon cross examination, the question I have repeated. Gentlemen, I did not ask that question without a reason, because in this very same paper to which I called your attention, and the attention of my learned friend during his address to you.

I found in staring capitals "DO YOU WANT TO MARRY? If you wish to make the acquaintance of a suitable partner for husband or wife, you can do so confidentially, through this matrimonial department. For full particulars send ten cents to Dr. Landis, for this strictly confidential examination circular."

Gentlemen of the jury, these are the marriages that are made in heaven, referred to by my learned friend. Marriages in heaven at ten cents apiece.

My learned friend was very particular, and very earnest in calling your attention to what he assumed to be a fact, that the District Attorney was obliged to seek the records of the State of Massachusetts. That State which burned the Quakers, and hung witches, for a precedent of this indictment, or that the indictment was taken from the records of that State.

Why, gentlemen of the jury, half a century ago, here in the city of Philadelphia, a man by the name of "Sharpless" was tried, and convicted by a jury of Philadelphians for the exhibtion of an obscene and lewd print, for the purpose of depraving and corrupting or inflaming the passions of the young to bad uses.

Gentlemen of the jury, that Seventeenth Massachusetts Report, to which my learned friend refers, as the volume from which this indictment was taken, never saw the light of day until nearly ten years after the trial of "Sharpless" and after the publication of the second volume of Sergeant and Rawle.

Gentlemen of the jury if this indictment be contrasted with the language of the indictment found here, and reported in our own books in the case of the Commonwealth vs. Sharpless you will see for yourselves precisely where the forms are contained.

And that conviction, gentlemen of the jury, took place in this commonwealth, and in this city, forty years before it was made an offence under our particular statute.

It was an offence at common law, as I told you in the beginning of this case, and it continued to be an offence at common law, and it is still an offence at common law, and is now made a statutory offence and the indictment is made under the statute, under the forms of indictments in use for centuries under the common law.

This indictment, gentlemen of the jury, charges, that certain persons, in being evil disposed persons, and designing. contriving and intending the morals as well of divers other citizens of this commonwealth to debauch and corrupt, and to raise and create in their minds inordinate and lustful desires, on the first day of March 1825, at the time aforesaid and within the jurisdiction of this court in a certain house there situated, unlawfully wickedly and scandalously did exhibit, and show for money to persons, to the inquest aforesaid unknown a certain lewd wicked scandalous infamous and obscene painting, representing a man in an obscene posture with a woman, to the manifest corruption and subversion of youth, of citizens, of the commonwealth and so forth.

Gentlemen of the jury, I have no hesitation in reading this aloud in the presence of any female who may be in this court house.

Because at the opening of this case his Honor delicately suggested that the ladies present might be notified that there was nothing requiring their attendance here to day, in order that they might relieve themselves from the exposure of an argument in a case like this, if any of them remained gentlemen of the jury, they must take the consequences. The act was their own, and it is not mine.

Now, gentlemen of the jury, there was an indictment for exhibiting a print, the print of a man in a posture which is called indecent and obscene posture, with a woman, to the manifest corruption and subversion of youth.

That indictment was tried, as I stated before, in the Mayor's court of the city of Philadelphia. It was removed to the Supreme court of the Commonwealth; the indictment was sustained, and the defendant was punished for that very offence, which, as I have said two or three times was an offence at common law.

Now, gentlemen of the jury, when you take this book out to read it for yourselves ; when you read that portion of it to which I shall direct your attention, I will ask you to put this question to yourselves : " Whether this book is anything more than placing in print what was contained upon that picture exhibiting a man and woman in an indecent posture.

You will find, gentlemen of the jury that this book, or that part of it to which I refer is simply that and nothing more. It is a description of that very picture, in point of fact for which the man, who exhibited it was confined and imprisoned.

My learned friend says it is truth; that there is nothing lewd in truth ; there is nothing which God and Nature have presented to mankind that can be regarded as obscene or is lustful in its influence to those who are pure minded.

Gentlemen of the jury, we are told by the highest authority that marriage is honorable, and the bed undefiled. But if that bed be spread in the market place, and if what transpires under the veil of night, and in the privacy of the marriage chamber were to be exhibited in the broad glare of noonday, upon our public streets, does my friend say that there would be nothing obscene or impure in that.

Does my learned friend say that there is

nothing in such an exhibition suited to inflame lustful passions of the youth? No, gentlemen, he cannot say it. He cannot say it.

There is a native modesty, thank God, in every man's heart that leads him away from the eyes of men upon such occasions as these.

If you can permit this book, gentlemen of the jury, to be circulated in this community; if there is nothing obscene in that description which I shall point out to you, and which you can read when you retire to your chamber. Then, gentlemen, there would he nothing at all obscene in constructing a model, arranged and moved by machinery, showing the palpitation of the heart, and going through these operations.

Gentlemen of the jury, I hope this *Progressive Christian Church* is not to carry us back to the age of Pompeii, when the genital organs were carved in stone, and exhibited over the doors of the houses of that faded city.

Now, gentlemen of the jury, a single word in relation to the motives which have influenced this man in the publication of this work.

You have a great deal of his giving away money or contibuting it to some cause, to what cause I do not know, of which there is not a particle of evidence and which would have here nothing to do with this case.

When you take up this newspaper you will find this book advertised as no medical book, no scientific book was ever advertised before in these great staring capitals. And when you read in this book the magnificent Doctor of Divinity offering a wager gentlemen a wager from this Doctor of Divinity, from the right reverend Bishop Landis, offering a wager of fifty thousand dollars that there is more information contained in this little book upon the subject of the Secrets of Generation than is contained in any other book in the world of a thousand pages.

Do you suppose gentlemen of the jury that such advertisements as these are intended for the public benefit. Do you find in this work anything of a scientific nature,

and that is to be distributed only among married men and married women. On the contrary gentlemen you will find upon its very first pages as I pointed out in my opening address that this book is a book that every male and female should read.—

This book must not lie about the house, but every male and female should read it, aye, gentlemen, your innocent daughters should read it, your innocent sons should read it.

The home circle must not be polluted by this book, and we are to have the spirit of universal concubinage spread abroad throughout this community.

Gentlemen of the jury, so far as the question of malice is concerned, if this book were to be published and advertised for sale, for the purpose of making money, and all the evidence in the case shows that it is so, there is malice in that; just as much malice as was shown in the case of the Commonwealth *vs* Sharpless, who exhibited his picture to the public for money in a single room, why, for that, gentlemen, there was a picture that could only be seen by those who sought the room in which it was exhibited. But here is a book that is advertised every week to 20,000 people according to the declaration of this defendant, a book upon the Secrets of Generation, not advertised as a scientific work, but as a book that every boy and girl should read; a book which my learned friend says he would be willing to read to his own children. This is the book, gentlemen, which is advertised in this paper, for sale to anybody who may choose to buy it.

Anybody who will remit to this Right Reverend Doctor of Divinity the sum of one dollar, through the post office. Now, gentlemen of the jury, I am not going to insult your intelligence; I am not going to doubt your morality; I am not going to suppose for a moment that you mean to stand by and justify this flagrant violation of law by any further remarks upon the subject of this obscene libel. I shall simply present it to you under the charge of the Court, and will ask you when you retire to your rooms to read and decide for yourselves.

CHARGE of JUDGE PIERCE

TO THE JURY, IN THE CASE OF

The Commonwealth vs. S. M. Landis. M. D.

———◆———

Gentlemen of the Jury :—The bill of indictment in this case, charges the defendant, in the first count with having printed and published an obscene book, and in the second count with having exposed for sale an obscene printed book. The act of assembly under which this indictment was found, is: If any person shall publish or sell any filthy and obscene libel, or shall expose for sale or exhibit or sell any indecent, lewd and obscene print, painting or statue, or if any person shall keep or maintain any house, room or gallery for the purpose of exposing or exhibiting any lewd indecent or obscene prints, pictures, paintings or statues, and shall be convicted thereof, such person shall be sentenced to pay a fine not exceeding five hundred dollars and undergo an imprisonment not exceeding one year. The object of this statute, Gentlemen of the Jury, is to preserve the purity of the public mind and to guard society against the issue, publication and sale of lewd and obscene prints, books, statues or paintings. We all understand somewhat, the nature of the human mind, and the influences to which it is subject.

I have no doubt, that the laws or our nature, which God has implanted within us, are wisely implanted for beneficial ends and purposes. We are endowed with reason and in the reasonable exercise of the natural laws and functions of our being, we are simply obeying the will of our Maker and carrying out those laws which He has placed in us for the purpose of good. But it frequently happens, as we know and are conscious that these wise laws of our being are perverted to wicked ends and purposes. They thus become violations of the law of God, violations of the high purposes for which they were implanted in us, and tend to mischief, to the destruction of society. Therefore the law of the land, and not what we think of the law of God, comes in to preserve the purity of society, by prohibition of these acts. It tends to observe these natural laws of our being and to preserve them for the wise ends and purposes for which they were created. Therefore, the law prohibits the publication or sale of anything which tends to excite in us wicked and lewd passions, and which tend to carry into our households to the injury of ourselves and our children those things which unnecessarily and improperly inflame the passions, wisely leaving the exercise of those laws of our being to proper times and under

4

legitimate circumstances, and seeking to allay passion, except under its proper surroundings and conditions.

Therefore if anything tends to inflame the mind and to unduly exercise or bring into operation lewd thoughts and feelings, the law punishes it as an offence against society. This indictment charges the defendant with having published and exposed for sale a book of this character; whilst the law punishes offences of this character, and libels which defame the living or the dead, at the same time it guards the rights of publication. By the constitution of the State of Pennsylvania, it is provided that printing presses should be free; and every citizen may freely speak, write and print on any subject, being responsible for the abuse of that liberty. And in all indictments for libel the jury shall have a right to determine the extent of the abuse as in other cases.

Now, gentlemen, in order to justify, a publication of this character you must be satisfied in your own minds that the publication was made for a legitimate and useful end and purpose; that it was not done from any wanton motive; any motive of mere gain, or with a corrupt desire to debauch society. It appears, that medical books treating of the subjects discussed in the book published by the defendant, are issued and sold in the market. And I have no doubt that such books, if discreetly published and placed in proper hands, have a useful purpose; but I have no doubt also that publications of a character which is strictly scientific, strictly medical, containing illustrations exhibiting the human form, if wantonly exposed in the public markets, and publicly advertised for sale in such a manner as to create a wanton and wicked desire for them, and not to promote the good of society by placing them in proper hands, that then such publications would be obscene and libelous.

Therefore, gentlemen, I say to you, no matter how true the things are which are published in this book; no matter how correct they may be, or in conformity with nature, or the laws of our being, or how correctly stated, that will not justify its publication; if it be in itself obscene, and tends to inflame improper and lewd passions and is published and sold for the purpose of making gain out of it, and not for the purpose of communicating proper information to persons who are entitled to know it, it is an improper publication. The determination of this question, therefore, does not depend upon whether the things published in the book are true or false, it may be just as obscene and libelous if true, as if it were false. You may readily understand this when I say that before a class of medical students, it might be necessary and exceedingly proper and consonant with decency and modesty, to expose a human body for the purpose of operation, or the exhibition of disease. But if the same human body were exposed in front of one of our medical colleges to the public indiscriminately, even for the purpose of operation, such an exhibition would be held to be indecent and obscene.

It might possibly be necessary, under some exigency, to exhibit the human body in court to a jury, to enable them to determine some question of fact. To do so in such a manner as to wantonly expose the body, to the public gaze, would be improper, but to give the jury an opportunity of viewing it in a private room, or in such a manner as not to expose it to the public gaze, would be eminently proper and becoming. So publication may be made of certain matters which are in themselves proper if properly published; but if they be wantonly and wickedly exposed and published, they become obscene and libelous.

With this discrimination, therefore, it matters not how correct and scientific the statements of this book are, the question for your consideration are, the purposes for which it was printed, the manner in which it was exposed for sale and offered to the public whether or not it was done for a lawful, legitimate and proper motive or for the purpose of making gain or for any other purpose not legitimate in itself.

In order to enable you to arrive at a correct conclusion upon this question, the paper called the *"Sharp Shooter"* has been given in evidence to enable you to know the motive which prompted the issue. In it the book called the "SECRETS OF GENERATION" which is the subject of this prosecution is publicly advertised, the price of it is given and the assertion in the advertisement is that it is for sale only by Dr. Landis at his office, corner of 13th and Girard Avenue, forwarded, sealed pre-paid by return mail upon receipt of price. Now gentlemen, there is an open and public offer of sale to anybody. A child of your family, or my family, a member of the family of any one in any distant part of the country; without regard to whether that person be male or female, married or single, a child of tender years or a person of mature life, may have the book, without regard to any of these circumstances, on payment of its price. This appears to be the case from the advertisement, and I suggest this view of it to you for your consideration.

This Book was open to any body and everybody who send for it, without regard to necessities of their case or their condition.

And then, gentlemen if upon an examination of the book you find that it is of a character to excite lewd desires and inflame the passions of men, no matter how correct the descriptions contained in it, are, or how accurate the science of the book is, it is within the offence prohibited by the act of assembly.

I am *very glad, for my own part that this prosecution has been instituted.* There are too many such books published, and if the public authorities have heretofore neglected the suppression of them, I am very glad to see that they are now beginning to take notice of them and action respecting them.

Nature takes care of itself in all questions of this character; it requires very little aid or explanation from man. God has implanted within us certain appetites which do not require much knowledge to enable us to exercise. A child almost as soon as it is born begins to recognize the feeling of hunger, and the sensations of heat and cold, or pain, if ten thousand books were written upon the subject, at first the child could not understand it and consequently he would not be much benefited. The necessities of our nature and our being will enable us to exercise the func-

tions. So with the other laws of our being. God when He created us gave us wants and appetites and functions to exercise, implanted within us also those instincts, those passions, those pains, those sensibilities, which lead us to the exercise of those functions without any very extensive instruction from anybody.

I think, therefore, that books of this character are not needed in society. If there be any difficulty in any case, by reason of disease, or mal-conformation, a proper medical adviser should be sought and advice taken respecting it; all other cases take care of themselves. But you will examine the book for yourselves, and not take my opinion of it, but take it from your own examination of it.

The great trouble is that there is too much exercise of power without any instructions from anybody; and it is as likely to be correctly exercised without instructions of this character as with them. If then you have the same opinion of this book that I have, you will condemn it. You will also find that this book contains directions respecting a matter which I think has become a fearful crime throughout the United States, that is, the manner of preventing the natural operation of the laws of our being, the prevention of conception or pregnancy.

In olden times almost every family consisted of ten or twelve children. It is one of my earliest recollections visiting my relatives in the country that each of their families consisted of not fewer than ten or twelve children, and my own good fortune is to have had ten children. Formerly every homestead was crowded with children, and they were usually a blessing to their parents, and society. But now, through some process of hindrance, such as is described in this book, families are dwarfed to one or two children, or three or four at the most. Thus society is hindered of its natural increase, and the health of women is endangered by the means of prevention and obstruction to the operation of natural laws

It is not necessary that I should prolong these remarks, if upon examination of this book, you should find that it contains matters which are obscene and tend only to inflame the passions of the young and old, and that it is not published for any wise, beneficial or useful purpose, but simply for the purpose of gain, without regard to whether it corrupts society or not, then it is a malicious libel.

I am requested to Charge you, that:—

"The Law will not presume a communication to have been through malice, which was made confidentially in good faith and in discharge of a legal, social or moral obligation and through benevolence to the public."

I affirm this point. The meaning of it is that if you are aware that anybody is doing an injury to another or anything calculated to do injury generally, and you give information respecting it in good faith, and in a proper manner, you are protected. But where this is done for the purposes of gain, for the purpose of making money without regard to the welfare of society and the communication itself tends to excite passion, and provoke obscenity, in such a case the law does not hold.

"If the production was honestly meant to inform the public mind and warn them against supposed dangers in society--though the subject may have been treated erroneously--then, however the Judgment of the Jury may incline them to think individually, they should acquit the defendant. If the Jury doubt of the criminal intention then also the law pronounces that he should be acquitted."

If the publication was proper to be made that is, gentlemen, if the injury is effected by the publication itself, then no matter how mistaken the party may have been in supposing he was doing good, he is within the law.

It does not do for men to imagine they are doing good, when they are doing things tending to injure and debauch society and to think that they are to be justified in their act because men happen to have a different opinion.

Again:

"A communication made bona fide upon any subject matter in reference to which he has a duty is privileged, if made to a person having a corresponding duty, although it contained criminating matter, which without this privilege would be slanderous and actionable."

That is so, gentlemen, for instance you have an unfaithful and dishonest servant in your house, and that servant applies for a situation to some other person, and that person desires to know the character of that servant—you are perfectly justified in such a case, in saying of that servant she is a thief, she has stolen my goods,—you have said it under a necessity, and you have stated the facts under our law. This would have been harder at all times as the law previously was, but some recent changes have been made and it cannot be so regarded at present, but if you fail to tell the truth and suffer them to take into their families dishonest domestics as in the meaning of this law you are not protected but would be liable.

Again:

"If the use to be attained is justifiable, as, if the object is generally to give useful information to the community, or to those who have a right and ought to know, in order that they may act upon such information, the occasion is lawful and the party may then justify or excuse the publication."

I affirm this point, subject to the remark I have just made.

"It is the undoubted right of every member of the community to publish his own opinions on all subjects of public and common interest, and so long as he exercises this inestimable privilege candidly, honestly and sincerely with a view to benefit society he is not amenable as a criminal.

But where public mischief is the object of the act and the means used are calculated to effect that object, the publication is noxious and injurious to society, and is therefore criminal."

I affirm that point, it is the point upon which I have been talking, where it is necessary in order to protect society from great mischief a publisher is protected but where the means to do this thing is in itself mischievous he is not protected.

"If the Jury find the teaching of this book calculated to benefit the persons to whom it is dedicated—they should acquit the Defendant."

Well gentlemen it may be under peculiar circumstances, that a person may derive benefit from the book, but placed indiscriminately in the hands of persons not requiring such advice and benefit, and it tends to inflame their minds, and is obscene in its character, then gentlemen it is not protected.

It is for you to determine the character of the book if in your judgment you think the book is fit and proper for the welfare of society, and that such a book as that ought to be published, and it is such as society demands, and ought to be to go into your families, to be handed to your sons and daughters and placed in boarding schools, and so forth, for general useful information, why then if that be the character of the book it is your duty to acquit the defendant.

"If the Jury believe the Defendant have in view the benefit of society—however wrong the ideas or objectionable the language—there is no malice and he should be acquitted."

Well, gentlemen, his ideas of wrong feelings or wrong influences of that thing is not the question.

The question is, is the thing in itself obscene and libelous, no matter what opinion he has. The malice of the thing would lie in the improper publication of it even under the mistaken view of the matter. But if you can abstract from the fact of the publication that the idea is gain, then malice may exist, and is evident from the mere fact of the publication of an improper book of this character, where the object is simply gain. Malice is *malus animus*. The attempt of any kind, for the purpose of gain, to throw broadcast on society firebrands or publications of any character tending to injure the welfare of society, is malicious.

It is not necessary that a man should have a malicious desire to render impure the fountains of life and corrupt the morals of society. It is not enough that his mind is in that condition which will forbid him to do an injury of this character; an avaricious man may not for the purpose of gain distribute things in society which are hurtful.

"If this Jury entertain a reasonable doubt either as to the obscenity of the book or the design of the defendant to injure society by the publication of this book, they should acquit him."

I charge you, gentlemen, whatever doubt you may have as to the obscenity of the book or to the design of the defendant, it goes properly to the defendant, that is if there be any such reasonable doubt in your mind as to render it uncertain, or to compel you to render a verdict that this is an obscene libellous book unfit for publication, why then that doubt is the property of the defendant, and it should go to his acquital.

It appears to be a fact, without doubt, that he was publishing the book and printing it for sale. The whole defence is not that he was not offering it for sale, but that he was not offering an obscene book. Therefore there can be no doubt as to the fact of the publication, offering the book for sale. If there be a doubt as to the obscenity of the book, then gentlemen, you must be clearly convinced, of the fact, and that doubt if there be such a doubt is the property of defendant.

But gentlemen when you look at the book you will be able to determine that question for yourselves, without any expression of opinion on my part at this point of the case.

If a doubt exists as to the design of the defendant to injure society, as I have already said that goes to his acquital. It is not his view as to what will injure society that is to determine his guilt or innocence, but the question of fact, as to whether this is an obscene libel, or not, but if you are convinced of it, no matter what may be his opinion, it is your duty to convict.

"If the design of the book was to benefit society it does not show malice to take measures to extend its circulatation."

I do not charge you that the design of it was to benefit society, but if you find the book, is calculated to benefit society, then there is no malice.

This subject I have already remarked upon. If it was the design of the publisher to benefit society, and he was mistaken, that does not interfere with the injury he does to society. He is guilty of an offence, but if the book is calculated to benefit society then gentlemen, it is not an obscene libel. If it is calculated to benefit society alone, and not to injure society, why then, gentlemen, it is not characterized as a libelous publication, but that is a question purely for your own examination of the book.

The Jury rendered a verdict of Guilty.

The Commonwealth | *In the Court of Oyer and Terminer and Quarter Sessions of the Peace for City and County of Philadelphia.*

vs.

Dr. Simon M. Landis. | *January Sessions, 1870.*

REASONS FOR A NEW TRIAL.

1.—The learned Judge erred in not allowing either of the following questions to be asked witnesses for defendant:

I. Is there a direct communication between the brain and genital organs?

II. What are uses of the genital organs? Are they ever abused through ignorance?

III. When these organs are abused, how is the brain affected?

IV. Does the healthy, natural use of the genital organs convey impurity to the mind?

V. Are diseases often caused by abusive sexual intercourse, especially in woman? name them.

VI. Are such conditions favorable to generate healthy offspring?

VII. Do you consider it proper to enlighten married persons upon the natural and proper use of the organs of generations?

VIII. Will this truth tend to improve or demoralize the community?

IX. Is it lawful, moral, and Godly to improve the human race as well as animals?

X. Are the morals of any human being impaired by a proper knowledge of the highest use of the sexual organs?

XI. Have you ever known a case where the inexperienced wife was injured through her husband's ignorance of the natural mode of producing conditions favorable to sexual intercourse?

XII. Does not the information given in this book complained of, have a tendency to prevent disease, exhalt the idea of marriage, and render more sacred sexual intercourse?

XIII. Does not the condition of the mother's mind at the time of conception, vitally affect the mental and physical organization of the child?

2.—The learned Judge erred in overruling the question : " Is that an obscene book ? " in language following, to-wit:

" I think the fact of its obscenity will manifest itself to any one, and it is not necessary to call an expert to prove that, and I overrule the offer to show such a fact?

3.—The learned Judge erred in overruling the question directed to the witness in these words—"Is this information proper to be given to the public by a Physician?"

4.—The learned Court erred in giving as a reason for overruling the above question—

That it was a question for the Jury—there being no evidence admitted upon which the Jury could pass respecting the question.

5.—The learned Court erred in charging the Jury in words following to wit:

"Now, gentlemen, in order to justify, a publication of this character you must be satisfied in your own minds that the publication was made for a legitimate and useful end and purpose ; that it was not done from any wanton motive ; any motive of mere gain, or with a corrupt desire to debauch society.

6.—The learned Judge erred in charging the Jury in the following language, viz :

"*I am very glad gentlemen, for my own part that this prosecution has been instituted.*" We have had a great abundance of publication of such books and I have been informed that many others are being published in this community, and if the thing has been neglected heretofore, it is high time, and I am very glad to see that the public authorities are beginning to take notice of it and action respecting it."

7.—The learned Court erred in using the following words in his charge to the jury—viz :

Therefore gentlemen although it is my thought, you are not to take my opinion, but take it from your own examination of that book. From your own sense of duty to yourself and to society. Therefore I think gentlemen that books of this character are not needed in society. If there be any difficulty in any case, by reason of disease, or mal-conformation or any thing of the kind, a proper medical adviser should be sought to advise respecting it, all other cases take care of themselves.

The great trouble is that there is too much excess of power in this direction without informatiom from anybody, without getting advice from anybody, and it is as much likely to be correctly done without any instructions of this character, as with them. If then you have the same opinion of this book that I have, you will condemn it, then gentlemen you will find that this book also contains directions respecting a matter which I think has become a fearful crime throughout the United States, that is the manner of preventing the natural operation of the laws of our being, the prevention of conception or pregnancy.

In olden times when every family consisted of ten or twelve children. I remember. and one of my earliest recollections is of visiting my relatives in the country, when each of them had no fewer than ten and some twelve. I have the good fortune to have ten children, and during the early period of my life, I remember every household and homestead was crowded with children, and they all tended to be a blessing to society and to parents. But to these latter times through some process or other, through some process of hindrance, such as are contained in this book, families are dwarfed to one or two children, or three or four at the most. Society hindered the health of women endangered by the prevention of the natural of laws our being in this respect and others."

8.—The learned Court erred as to the first point when asked to judge, on behalf of defendant. that

"The Law will not presume a communication to have been through malice, which was made confidentially in good faith and in discharge of a legal, social or moral obligation and through benevolence to the public."

in neither denying or affirming the same, but in using the following language, to wit:

" That is so, gentlemen, but the meaning of it is that if you are aware that anybody is doing an injury to another, and anything calculated to do injury generally, and you give information respecting that in good faith, and in a proper manner, you are protected. But where this is alone for the purpose of making money, without regard to the welfare of society, and the communication itself tends to excite passion, and provoke obscenity, why then in such a case the law does not hold."

9.—The learned Court erred, as to the second point when he was asked to charge, the jury on behalf of defendant, that

"If the production was honestly meant to inform the public mind and warn them against supposed dangers in society—though the subject may have been treated erroneously—then, however the Judgment of the Jury may incline them to think individually, they should acquit the defendant. If the Jury doubt of the criminal intention then also the law pronounces that he should be acquitted."

in neither denying or affirming the same, but in using the following language to wit:

" Well, if the publication was proper to be made, that is so, gentlemen ; but if the injury is effected by the publication itself, then no matter how mistaken the party may have been in supposing he was doing a good he is within the law.

It does not do for men to imagine they are doing good, when they are doing things tending to injure and debauch society, and to think that they are to be justified in their act because men happen to have a different opinion."

10.—The learned Court erred as to the third point he was asked to charge the jury on behalf of defendant, that

"A communication made bona

fide upon any subject matter in reference to which he has a duty is privileged, if made to a person having a corresponding duty, although it contained criminating matter, which without this privilege would be slanderous and actionable."

in neither denying or affirming the same, but in using the following language to wit:

That is so. gentlemen, for instance you have an unfaithful and dishonest servant in your house, and that servant applies for a situation to some other person, and that person desires to know the character of that servant—you are perfectly justified in such a case, in saying of that servant she is a thief. she has stolen my goods,—you have said it under a necessity, and you have stated the facts under our law. This would have been harder at all times as the law previously was, but some recent changes have been made and it cannot be so regarded at present, but if you fail to tell the truth and suffer them to take into their families dishonest domestics as in the meaning of this law you are not protected but would be liable.

11.—The learned Court erred as to the *fourth* point, when asked to charge on behalf of defendant that

"If the use to be attained is justifiable, as, if the object is generally to give useful information to the community, or to those who have a right and ought to know, in order that they may act upon such information, the occasion is lawful and the party may then justify or excuse the publication."

in saying "it is so, subject to the remark I have just made.

12.—The learned Court erred as to the *fifth* point, when asked to charge on behalf of defendant that

"It is the undoubted right of every member of the community to publish his own opinions on all subjects of public and common interest, and so long as he exercises this inestimable privilege candidly, honestly and sincerely with a view to benefit society he is not amenable as a criminal.

But where public mischief is the object of the act and the means used are calculated to effect that object,

the publication is noxious and injurious to society, and is therefore criminal."

in using the following words:

I affirm that point, it is the point upon which I have been talking, where it is necessary in order to protect society from great mischief a publisher is protected but where the means to do this thing is in itself mischievous he is not protected.

13.—The learned Court erred as to the sixth point when asked to charge the jury on behalf of defendant that

"If the Jury find the teaching of this book calculated to benefit the persons to whom it is dedicated—they should acquit the Defendant."

in neither affirming nor denying the same. but in using the following words:

Well gentlemen it may be under peculiar circumstances, that a person may derive benefit from the book, but placed indiscriminately in the hands of persons not requiring such advice and benefit, and it tends to inflame their minds, and is obscene in its character, then gentlemen it is not protected.

It is for you to determine the character of the book if in your judgment you think the book is fit and proper for the welfare of society, and that such a book as that ought to be published, and it is such as society demands, and ought to be to go into your families, to be handed to your sons and daughters and placed in boarding schools, and so forth, for general useful information, why then if that be the character of the book it is your duty to acquit the defendant.

14.—The learned Court erred as to the seventh point when asked to charge the jury on behalf, of defendant, that

"If the Jury believe the Defendant have in view the benefit of society—however wrong the ideas or objectionable the language—there is no malice and he should be acquitted."

in neither affirming nor denying the same, but in using the following words:

Well, gentlemen, his ideas of wrong feelings or wrong influences of that thing is not the question.

The question is, is the thing in itself obscene and libelous, no matter what opinion he has. The malice of the thing would lie in the improper publication of it even under the mistaken view of the matter. But if you can abstract from the fact of the publication that the idea is gain, then malice may exist, and is evident from the mere fact of the publication of an improper book of this character, where the object is simply gain. Malice is *malus animus*. The attempt of any kind, for the purpose of gain, to throw broadcast on society firebrands or publications of any character tending to injure the welfare of society, is malicious.

It is not necessary that a man should have a malicious desire to render impure the fountains of life and corrupt the morals of society. It is not enough that his mind is in that condition which will forbid him to do an injury of this character; an avaricious man may not for the purpose of gain distribute things in society which are hurtful.

15.—The learned Court erred as to the eighth point when asked to charge the jury on behalf of the defendant, that

"If this Jury entertain a reasonable doubt either as to the obscenity of the book or the design of the defendant to injure society by the publication of this book, they should acquit him."

in neither affirming nor denying the same, but in using words as follows, viz:

I charge you, gentlemen, whatever doubt you may have as to the obscenity of the book or to the design of the defendant, it goes properly to the defendant, that is if there be any such reasonable doubt in your mind as to render it uncertain, or to compel you to render a verdict that this is an obscene libellous book unfit for publication, why then that doubt is the property of the defendant, and it should go to his acquittal.

It appears to be a fact, without doubt, that he was publishing the book and printing it for sale. The whole defence is not that he was not offering it for sale, but that he was not offering an obscene book. Therefore there can be no doubt as to the fact of the publication, offering the book for sale. If there be a doubt as to the obscenity of the book, then gentlemen, you must be clearly convinced, of the fact, and that doubt if

there be such a doubt is the property of defendant.

But gentlemen when you look at the book you will be able to determine that question for yourselves, without any expression of opinion on my part at this point of the case.

If a doubt exists as to the design of the defendant to injure society, as I have already said that goes to his acquital. It is not his view as to what will injure society that is to determine his guilt or innocence, but the question of fact, as to whether this is an obscene libel, or not, but if you are convinced of it, no matter what may be his opinion, it is your duty to convict.

16.—The learned Court erred as to the ninth point when asked to charge the jury on behalf of defendant, that

"If the design of the book was to benefit society it does not show malice to take measures to extend its circulatation."

in neither affirming nor denying the same, but in using the following words:

I do not charge you that the design of it was to benefit society, but if you find the book, is calculated to benefit society, then there is no malice.

This subject I have already remarked upon. If it was the design of the publisher to benefit society, and he was mistaken, that does not interfere with the injury he does to society. He is guilty of an offence, but if the book is calculated to benefit society then gentlemen, it is not an obscene libel. If it is calculated to benefit society alone, and not to injure society, why then, gentlemen, it is not characterized as a libelous publication, but that is a question purely for your own examination of the book.

17.—The verdict was against the evidence and the weight of evidence.

18.—The verdict was against the law.

DAMON Y. KILGORE,
Att'y for Defendant.

PHILADELPHIA, January 17, 1870.

ARGUMENT

IN SUPPORT OF A MOTION FOR A

NEW TRIAL,

BEFORE

Hon. Wm. S. Peirce, Associate Justice,

By Damon Y. Kilgore, Esq.,

JANUARY 21, 1870.

MAY IT PLEASE YOUR HONOR:

The human mind is not perfect. It is finite and therefore liable to err. Belief does not depend upon volition, but upon the evidence presented, and the capability of the mind to appreciate or weigh that evidence Be it desirable or otherwise, whenever the evidence is sufficient to overcome former opinions or prejudices, the result is inevitable; our belief of yesterday, gives place to a higher one to-day.

In appearing before your Honor, to ask you to review your decision of but yesterday; and as a magistrate, and as a man, (for a man is greater than a magistrate) to pronounce upon your own handiwork.

I should hesitate to say what I am about to say, did I not place a higher estimate upon your Honor's integrity and candor, than the majority of mankind. Most men are slow to acknowledge and mend their own faults; though quick to see the faults of others. However erroneous may have been your Honor's decision on several points involved in this case, I am sure your high sense of duty to yourself, society, and this defendant, will outweigh all considerations of personal popularity or pride; and that you will pass your own work in review with a conviction and consciousness of being in the presence of that Great Judge from whose decision there is no appeal.

This is no ordinary case. It involves not only the liberty of the citizen, but the liberty of the press, in this age and in this country, where that liberty is guarded by the jealous interest of all the people.

The SECRETS OF GENERATION, which you call obscene, was written to promote the happiness of families, by teaching men and women the highest practical lessons of morality and virtue. It was written to enable them, in obedience to the laws of God, to become fathers and mothers of a nobler race. This book teaches the science of human life, its origin and perfection. It was written and published by this defendant with as pure a motive as ever inspired a human being. In this faith I ask your Honor to reverse the decision you have made, in condemnation of a book, containing truths of the highest interest to those who will come after us, and who as a higher court, will review our acts to day.

I said this case was important, because it had to do with *principles.* Men pass away. Generations are as shadows but principles are eternal. With the most profound personal respect for the Court, as well as the highest confidence in your Honor's endeavor to rise above all political, social or religious prejudice in the decision of this question, I shall speak plainly and without reserve.

My learned colleague took the ground in his able opening for the defence, that this book called the Secrets of Generation was a strictly *scientific and medical work* and as such, by the law, is *privilged*. We repeatedly urged that what would be wrongs in a newspaper, Byron, Pope or Shakspeare, is neither obscene nor objectionable in a work like this—a work under the seal of privacy—sold only to married persons, written by a physician upon physiological and hygienic laws. This was of vital importance to this defendant, and as I think improperly overlooked by your Honor in your charge to the jury.

The first reason for new trial, or in support of the motion for a rule to show cause why this question should not come before the Court in Banc, is the error of the learned Court in not allowing either of the foregoing questions to be asked witnesses for the defence. These questions, which I will not repeat, were carefully prepared by me to show the correctness and value of the *Secrets of Generation*. They are based upon medical science, as it is understood to day by scientific, medical men, and I think it was error not to allow them to be put.

The jury, being neither scientific nor medical men, were entirely incompetent to pass upon the contents of a medical book. The evidence of medical men as experts should have been allowed as to whether the "Secrets of Generation" was a scientific or medical work, because if so, the law is changed respecting it—grants to it certain immunities withheld from mere literary productions—makes it a *privileged work*. This testimony should have been allowed also to prove the *truth* of the principles enunciated in the book, and their importance to the human family. And although your Honor was particular to tell the jury you thought it use less, and that its tendency was to do more mischief than good to society; and although the jury might have come to the same conclusion, still it was the defendant's right, under the law, to have its benefits shown and I submit *medical men were the proper persons to weigh those benefits.*

If your Honor will notice the parts complained of, under the head "How and When to Generate Healthy and Talented Babies," you will see that after referring to

what science has demonstrated within the last hundred years, in reference to the improvement of animals, the defendant states how much more important it is for us to know the laws of nature respecting a right generation of human beings, and what those laws are. Touching that very point, I propounded the question " *Is there a direct communication between the brain and genital organs?*" To a superficial mind this question might seem irrelevant, but it went directly to the heart of this case. If I had shown there was such an intimate relation between the brain and the genital organs, that the state or condition of the brain at the time of conception, stamped the child with that condition, whether good or bad throughout his earthly life, it would have corroborated the statements of Dr. Landis, in the chapter most complained of. I asked the question " What are the uses of the genital organs?" in order to show that their highest and normal use is the production of human beings—starting in its career of life, a human soul. We should have shown further by the questions which followed that these organs were frequently abused through ignorance of the very facts contained in the Secrets of Generation, written by this defendant.

We should have shown further, that when these organs are abused, the brain is affected, and incalculable evils result to the race in consequence. All this testimony would have justified the publication of this book; upon *humanitarian grounds* and thus it would have borne upon the *motive* of Doctor Landis; for after all this man's guilt or innocence, is to be determined by two questions. 1. Is the Secrets of Generation an obscene book? And as the jury simply sustained your Honor's opinion of it. 2. What were the defendant's *motives* in publishing it? If there was no malice, there could have been no guilt. To constitute a libel, there must be some wicked intent, some malice expressed or implied. Without actual or constructive malice, you can not convict this defendant under the law, no matter how obscene the book might be. The Commonwealth will not, for a moment, contend that there is any express malice, and we desire to show there can be no constructive malice in a case like this. I now call your Honor's attention to "THE PHYSICAL LIFE OF WOMEN, *containing advice to the maiden, wife and mother,*" written by Dr. George H. Napheys of this city. In this book, I find testimonials, of its high character, from some of the most distinguished Doctors of Medicine and Doctors of Divinity (a sickly divinity that needs medicine) known throughout the land. William A. Hammond late Surgeon-General of the United States Army, says he hopes "it will reach every woman in the land." Horace Bushnell D. D. of Hartford, whose late effort against giving woman the ballot should give his opinion weight with all conservatives in their dotage, says "this book will be a great help." I see also the names of "Rev. George Alexander Crooke D. D., D. C. L.; Rev. George Bringhurst, Rector of the P. E. Church of the Messiah; the Librarian of the Philadelphia Library and the Ex-Principal of the Phiadelphia High School. I bought this book of a woman canvasser more to encourage her in self support than for anything contained in the book.

I did not know until this morning that it contained almost precisely the same information, given in the SECRETS OF GENERATION. This Author in speaking of animals says, on page 130. "If you wish to produce "females, give the male at the first signs of "heat; if you wish males, give him at the "end of the heat."

"Dr. Napheys applies this law to the "human race and quotes Dr. Packman's "statements, published in the *London Lancet,* that "in the human female, conception "in the first half of the time between "menstrual periods produces female off-"spring, and male in the latter." He quotes also from the *Philadelphia Medical* and *Surgical Reporter* for *February* 8 1868, to prove the truth of this law. He speaks of the improvement of animals by knowledge of these laws of procreation, and urges the application of science to generation of human beings, as a matter of "national concern."

MR DWIGHT.—I think we have some right to confine our friends to the theme of discussion. I do not think it turns upon some other book which contains the same facts, but whether or not the jury have the power to determine. I think it is improper and I object to it, because we have got to answer this, and we have the right to demand to answer only those things which are legitimate to it.

MR. KILGORE.—The point to which the learned assistant District Attorney referred is not the one now under discussion. I am now showing legitimately and properly, that the Judge erred in not allowing these questions which had a direct bearing upon the very heart of the defence, to be asked our witnesses. And I can assure that gentleman, he will get through with this case much sooner if he will leave out these childish objections.

I asked the question, whether diseases of women, were not caused through ignorance on the part of husbands of the very truths contained in the SECRETS OF GENERATION. This was ruled out. Your Honor referred to the fact that there was too great exercise of power in this direction, and we designed to prove that in consequence of this excess of power, used unwisely and ignorantly, the information in Dr. Landis' book was needed and that it would do incalculable good, in wisely directing this power.

The District Attorney complains that Dr. Landis, in striving to prevent these evils, has given instruction in reference to the proper *conditions* for the consummation of the marital relation. He does not say the instruction is not natural, that it is not true, but it is "obscene," and leaves a question of the highest importance to women, and to generations yet unborn, to be decided by an ignorant jury, without allowing one particle of light to be thrown upon the subject by medical experts, who above all others should be competent witnesses in this matter.

Dr. Napheys says, on page 70, "It some-"times happens that marriage is consumma-"ted with difficulty. To overcome this, care, "management and forbearance should al-"ways be employed, and anything like pre-"cipitation and violence avoided. Only the "consequences of unrestrained impetuosity "are to be feared. Violence then can only "be productive of injury and is not without "danger."

On page 115, in giving directions, "*how to have beautiful children,*" this author says—"To obtain this desired end, conception "should take place, only when both parents

" are in the best physical condition, at the
" proper season of the year, and with *mutual*
" *passion.* The body of the child can be in-
" fluenced by the mind of the parent, par-
" ticularly the mother "

We endeavored to prove by these questions
that the information in the SECRETS OF GEN-
ERATION, published by Dr. Landis, was
needed and that it was calculated to do
great good. In corroboration of the truth of
this position, which your Honor denied in
your charge to the Jury, I again quote from
this book which has been so highly recom-
mended not to *married persons* only, but for
general circulation.

On page 69 this Author says, "THE
" GREAT OBJECT OF THE CONJUGAL UNION IS
" THE TRANSMISSION OF LIFE.—*a duty necessary in order to repair the constant rava-
" ges of death, and thus perpetuate the race.
" In the fulfilment of this sublime obligation
" woman plays the more prominent part, as she
" is the source and depositary of the future
" being. It is of moment, therefore that she
" should not be ignorant of the nature and re-
" responsibilities of her position.* IGNORANCE
" HERE MEANS SUFFERING, DISEASE AND SOME-
" TIMES DEATH. *Let us then interrogate
" science in regard to these matters, among
" the most interesting of all human concerns.*"

Noble words, Doctor Napheys! Precise-
ly the ideas and almost the same language,
Dr. Landis published in the SECRETS OF
GENERATION, four years ago.

The questions which your Honor ruled out
were relevant in determining the character
of the book—whether it was obscene or not
and whether its teaching was true and fit
for publication. They were relevant in
determining the *motive* of the defendant,
even if the book, was not fit for publication
and general circulation.

COURT.—Have the jury not a right to
determine from the book itself whether it
was an obscene libel or not?

It was wholly inadequate whether the
facts stated were true or false; admitting it
to be right, if it was not a subject fit for
publication and general circulation, as has
not been proved in this case, as has been
done by Doctor Landis, why then it was an
obscene libel if it proceeded from a malicious motive, but they were to determine
that question from the evidence in the
case. I may probably admit to day the
correctness of the positions for which you

contend here, if all the facts be true.

MR. KILGORE.—Then the law is mistaken
your Honor, for I have it here.

COURT.—I put several cases in point,
one of an exposure before a medical class,
and another in the street which would
have been indecent.

MR. KILGORE.—I will answer that point
presently.

COURT.—You do not propose to say that
such an exposure would not be indecent.

MR. KILGORE.—No sir. But that has no
application to this case.

These questions refer to medical science,
and the well known maxim in law of
Quique sua arte credendum, permits these
medical gentlemen " to be examined on
questions of art and science, peculiar to their
trade or profession," as was ruled in the case
of Winans v. N. Y. & Erie R. R. Co., 21,
Howard's Reports, p. 88.

Your Honor took the law which applies to
this case entirely away from it, and had you
followed the well settled decisions upon that
point, and others, this defendant would never
have been convicted.

Had we been permitted to prove to the
jury the true character of this book—the necessity for its publication and the amimus of
the author, by the nineteen medical gentlemen who were ready to swear that it is not
obscene, there was not a man on that jury
who would have dared to convict Dr. Landis, unless he did it out of respect to the
Court.

COURT.—They very seldom do that.

MR. KILGORE.—I think they did in this
case, your Honor.

In charging the jury, you stated that there
was a heinous crime practiced in the community—the crime of preventing conception.
If your Honor please, this is a great mistake.
The difficulty is, there is not prevention
enough. Not only are men and women becoming physically weak, but they are also
becoming corrupt, especially in the large
cities.

Our modern civilization not only substi
tutes carbonic acid gas for pure air, but our
fashionable women are mere ornamental
dolls, incapable of mental or physical labor,
living aimless and worse than useless lives

because it is etiquette for them to do so. If they have children, it is vulgar to exercise over them a mother's care, and thus nine-tenths of all the children of wealth are turned over to the tender mercies of ignorant nurses to be spoiled before they come from the nursery.

For the laboring classes, it is an absolute necessity to prevent having children, because the times are so hard it is impossible for parents to support and educate large families. At this time it is a struggle for life with many parents in consequence of our ignorant and venal legislation, in favor of gigantic corporations and against the interests of all who labor—making the rich richer and the poor poorer. Ah, sir, these people who have been reared in luxury, have little sympathy with those starving with hunger and pinched with cold, whose necessities compel them to prevent having children and who often resort to the crime of abortion, because they are unable to support those they already have. Dr. Landis tells them that prevention is infinitely better than abortion. He tells them that if they will gratify their passions, it is better to prevent conception by *natural* means, than to generate unwelcome children, into whose very souls is organized the mothers hate; children of disease and lust, who by Nature's law, develope into criminals. He tells women not to use drugs which jeopardize their lives, but to follow Nature's laws in preventing the generation of that life they would afterwards seek to destroy. Thus he warns people against a sin which has become so common in fashionable and aristocratic life; a crime so entrenched within the pale of respectability in Church and State, that it already threatens American civilization.

In these views, this defendant does not stand alone. His position is sustained by all the best writers on this subject on both continents. Doctor Napheys after devoting ten pages to the prevention of conception, winds up the argument as follows—

"Should our position be attacked, how- " ever, the medical man must know that in "opposing our views, he opposes those of " the most distinguished physicians in this " country and in Europe; and the theologian " should be warned that when a neglect " of physical laws leads to moral evil, the " only way to correct this evil is to remedy " the neglect. In this case the neglect is in " over-production,—*the evil is abortion.*"

Doctor E. B. Foote, in his book entitled SOCIAL LIFE, published this year by Wells and Company of New York, says on page 576, "considering the incontrovertible facts " that many people, in consequence of "constitutional ill-health, inherited scrofula, " family predisposition to insanity, indigen- " cy; or of too rapid child bearing, should be " provided with means for regulating or "restraining procreation, it is surprising that "anybody possessing a thimble full of " sense, who is not impotent, should question " for a moment the propriety, nay, *the ne- " cessity* of informing the people as to the " best means science has yet devised for the " purpose."

COURT.—The command to multiply, and increase and replenish the earth was given to Adam and Eve. It does not hold now?

MR. KILGORE.—Yes sir—it is in force now. But God did not command people to multiply criminals; to replenish the earth with licentious and intemperate children. He spake to our first parents as he made them free from the diseases and excesses of modern civilization. He desires healthy people, who live in accordance with natural laws, to obey the same command now. My client says the same thing. The reason he objects to some people carrying out that command is, they transmit their own wicked desires and evil propensities; their imper-fections and impurities to their offspring and thus render life to them a curse, rather than a blessing.

Why sir, look at the great number of charities around Philadelphia for the sup-port of those who are unable to take care of themselves. If the advice of Dr. Landis were followed, such institutions would be superflous, because all would have enough to satisfy their wants.

I now pass to the second point, viz. "*The learned Judge erred in overruling the question "is that an obscene book?"* in language following to wit: "*The fact of its obscenity will manifest itself to any one.*" I submit, your Honor, this was really, the Judge taking the question of fact out of the hands of the jury and deciding the question for them. They were bound to convict under such ruling; it would have been disrespect to the Court to have acquitted this defendant. If your Honor's integrity did not stand so high in the opinion of your fellow citizens, such a remark would not be so dangerous—but so above suspicion is your Honor's character that your words have great weight, and to pass your opinion upon the fact as to whether or not the SECRETS OF GENERATION is obscene, in presence of the jury is dangerous to liberty and the rights of every citizen.

COURT.—In the Supreme Court in a case of homicide, involving life and death, the Judge may express his opinion as to the evidence and as to whether the facts made out the case, leaving it however to the jury to determine for themselves.

MR. KILGORE.—But that is not going as far as you went in this case. It is proper for the Court to say if you believe such and such facts, then it is your duty to convict or to acquit as the case may be. I do not think the Court has any right to go any further.

MR. GIBBONS.—It is done every day in this Court.

COURT.—I think at one time during the trial of homicides in Philadelphia that there were no convictions, and the judges held a Court of Oyer and Terminer and expressed most emphatic opinions with happy results.

MR. KILGORE.—I have no doubt it is necessary sometimes for judges to speak pointedly in regard to the bearing of certain facts—but it is not according to law for judges to decide facts which belong to the jury. If courts have that right, juries are superfluous.

IN REGARD TO THE THIRD REASON—I think the court erred in overruling the question, "*Is this information proper to be given to the public by a physician?*" This is a question going directly to the gist of the offence charged against this defendant. The law says:

In a criminal prosecution for a libel, "the " defendant may repel the charge by proving " that the publication was for a justifiable " purpose, and not malicious, nor with the " intention to defame any man. And there " may be many cases where the defendant " having proved the purpose justifiable, may

" give in evidence the truth of the words, " when such evidence will tend to negative " the malice and intent to defame." *Commonwealth vs Clapp*, 4 *Mass.*, 163.

As his book is a medical book, written by a physician, upon the laws of health, this defendant had a right to prove, by the only persons competent to testify on the subject, that the information contained in the book was proper to be given to the public by a physician. And if we had proved that, and also that the book was calculated to do good, he could not have been convicted. Again, the laws says:

" Every wilful and unauthorized publica- " tion injurious to the character of another, is " a libel; but when the writer is acting upon a " duty, legal or moral, towards the person to " whom he writes, or is bound by his situation " to protect the interest of such person, that " which he writes under such circumstances " is a *privileged* communication unless the " writer be actuated by malice. *Cockayne & Hodgkinson*, 5 *Car. & Pa.*, 543.

" A privileged work means nothing more " than that the occasion of making it rebuts " the *prima facia* inference of malice arising " from the publication of matter prejudicial " to the character of the plaintiff, and throws " upon him the onus of proving malice in " fact." *Wright & Woodgate*, 2 *Crompton, Meeson & Roscoe*, 573.

The Supreme Court of the United States, decided that " Wherever the author or pub- " lisher of the alleged slander acted in the " bona fide discharge of a public or private " duty, legal or moral" such communication " is privileged. *White & Nicholls*, 3 *Howard* 267.

" The rule of evidence, as to such cases " is so changed as to require the plain- " tiff to bring home to the defendant, the ex- " istence of malice, as the true motive of his " conduct." *Ibid*.

" As the offence of publishing a libel con- " sists in the malicious publication of it, " which as already stated, is in general in- " ferred from the words of the alleged libel " itself, it is competent to the defendant *in* " *all cases*, to show the absence of malice on " his part." *Roscoe's Criminal Evidence*, 538.

Again, the learned Court erred in saying it was a question for the jury to determine from the evidence when every particle of testimony on the subject had been ruled out.

In saying in your charge, "*I am very glad gentlemen for my own* part, that this prose- cution has been instituted," I think your Honor committed a grievous error It was calculated greatly to prejudice this defendant in the minds of the jury. If such expressions are tolerated from Judges, then farewell to the rights of defendants in trial by jury—farewell to liberty and justice. At some future time, not far distant, a Jeffreys might occupy that seat you now honor, and as public prosecutors are always the tools of power, it might come to pass, that he would attempt to put out of the way of his own ambition every honest man who opposed him, and with such a Judge and such precedents it could easily be done.

COURT.—In Kilpatrick's case, the Supreme Court decided that "a Judge may rightfully express his opinion respecting the evidence, and it may sometimes be his duty to do it, yet not so as to withraw it from the consideration and decision of the jury.

MR. KILGORE.—Exactly. That is just what we say, but what we complain of is, your Honor did so express yourself as to withdraw the vital points in the case for the consideration and decision of the jury. Your Honor left nothing for the jury to do.

COURT.—The book may be true to the very letter and yet it may be obscene.

MR. KILGORE.—If it be obscene, and is truth the law acquits the defendant.

COURT.—Suppose it were a painting exhibiting any human being, every line of which was true, every particle of the organism depicted and then it should be advertised in a room for anybody to see for 25 cents that is an obscene libel.

MR. KILGORE.—Do I understand your honor, to intimate that there would be any difference in the act whether it was gratuitous or whether 25 cents was charged for the right?

COURT.—So I understand it.

MR. KILGORE.—I noticed this morning on my way here a beautiful cast in plaster, representing the human female naked, in a window on Chestnut street. In the Academy of Fine Arts, women are paid to go and expose their bodies naked as they were born, and artists of both sexes go there to draw pictures of their bodies from nature.

COURT.—I do not think there is anything of the kind done.

MR. KILGORE.—But it is true your Honor, nevertheless.

The learned Court erred in using the following words :

Therefore I think gentlemen that books of this character are not needed in society. If there be any difficulty in any case, by reason of disease, or mal-conformation or any thing of the kind, a proper medical adviser should be sought to advise respecting it, all other cases take care of themselves.

The great trouble is that there is too much excess of power in this direction without informatiom from anybody, without getting advice from anybody, and it is as much likely to be correctly done without any instructions of this character, as with them. If then you have the same opinion of this book that I have, you will condemn it, etc.

Now if your Honor please, your opinion as to whether or not this book is needed, should never have gone into that jury box. Neither should you have said to the jury "*if you have the same opinion of this book that I have,* YOU WILL CONDEMN IT."

That one expression was enough to make the jury condemn the book. And yet I could have proved just the opposite by nineteen physicians had they been permitted to testify.

MR. GIBBONS.—I do not think your Honor is responsible for the bad English he has been quoting.

MR. KILGORE.—And the bad law I hope your Honor will correct for the benefit of the District Attorney.

I have shown by the latest and best medical works, that this information *is needed* in society. Doctor Landis, has felt the importance of giving the people light on these subjects, for many years.

The District Attorney objected to some of the terms used by the Doctor.

MR. GIBBONS.—Will you allow me to correct you—I did not object to any particular word.

MR. KILGORE.—He marked a few sentences which he regards as obscene. The jury did not read a hundreth part of the book. As it was all put in evidence, we had the right to have it taken as a whole. I do not think any honest, pure minded man, can read the entire book without being convinced that the Author's motive in writing it was good.

Some few passages on this book, as well as in the Bible may be found objectionable but the whole spirit and tenor of the book, dispels every impure thought.

The book taken as a whole would never have convicted him.

COURT.—The juries are very queer, they do not care much for the Judge nor any one else.

MR. KILGORE—That is the best evidence that they needed the testimony of the best experts to inform them on difficult points.

COURT.—It was not the same kind of information they needed as in your case.

MR. KILGORE.—I noticed the District Attorney stood aside a great number of working men in selecting the jury, and I inferred, he was trying to get men of leisure, *retired gentlemen,* who have no business, who would be pretty sure to convict this defendant. Idleness is the parent of crime—the devil always finds plenty of work for idle hands to do.

MR. GIBBONS.—I do not like to interrupt my friend, but there was not a man on the jury who was not a respectable, working man, not one.

MR. KILGORE.—I noticed he never stood aside any except working men—and he appeared very anxious to get those described as *gentlemen.* However it is possible he is not quite so bad as I supposed.

I now come to consider those points of law we asked your Honor to affirm in your charge to the Jury.

When requested to charge that,

" The Law will not presume a communi-
" cation to have been through malice, which
" was made confidentially in good faith and
" in discharge of a legal, social or moral obli-
" gation and through benevolence to the pub-
" lic,"

If you had simply said, I affirm that point the jury would have acquitted this defendant. But you said—" That is so gentlemen, but the meaning of it is that if you are aware that anybody is doing an injury to another, and anything calculated to do injury generally, and you give information respecting that in good faith, and in a proper manner, you are protected. But where this is alone for the purpose of mak-

ing money, without regard to the welfare of society, and the communication itself tends to excite passion, and provoke obscenity, why then in such a case the law does not hold. '

This language was calculated to mislead the jury. It was calculated to strengthen the false position taken by the District Attorney—that the Doctor's description of copulation for useful ends was as obscene as the lewd picture shown by Sharpless for money, without any design to benefit anybody. The "Sharp-Shooter" was put in evidence to prove money was the object and purpose of publishing this book, and not " benevolence to the public." The distinction between medical or privileged works and such vile trash as was sold by Scroggy, was entirely overlooked. The District Attorney argued that because the SECRETS OF GENERATION were advertised for sale, it was *prima facie* evidence that the sole purpose of this defendant in publishing it, was *mere gain,* and your Honor everywhere in your charge, strengthened this view of the Commonwealth's offi. cer. You also took it for granted because the book was advertised for sale by letter through the post office, that children could purchase it, which was not true. Dr. Landis always carefully guarded its sale, so that it never went into the hands of children.

No malice was proved, because none existed and it was contrary to law to presume it.

Constructive malice can only exist where the act itself is so wicked that the *safety of society* requires that the doer should be punished as if he were malicious, or where it would be impossible for a person to do so wrong an act unless he was actuated by malice. Now sir, no one will pretend this applies to the Author of SECRETS OF GENERATION.

The District Attorney has referred to the common law respecting libel.

Why sir, it has always been regarded a great offence. By the Roman law it was punished with great severity, and I think the twelve tables made it a capital offence. Libel is derived from the Latin word *libellus,* which signifies a little book. In the criminal law of the Romans the word *famosus* which signifies scandalous or malicious, was used to specify the kind of

5

book which the law condemned. In accurate legal documents in England the expression *libellus famosus* is translated defamitory writing.

Lord Chancellor Lyndhurst said he never met with a definition of libel which exactly suited him. In "The People vs Croswell," 3 Johnson's cases, 354 I find the following definition of a libel. "A censorious or ridiculous writing, picture or sign, made with a mischievous and malicious intent toward government, magistrates, or individuals."

In no law book, from the time the word was first used, is there an instance where *malice* did not enter into a libel. The definition I have just read, is approved in 9 Johnson's Reports 214, and more recently in Denio's Reports 347.

Now sir the essence of the offence of libel lies in its being *dangerous to the public peace.*

Precisely on the same foundation as slander, with this distinction, that the law considers that words, which while only spoken, are fleeting and transitory, become fixed and permanent by publication, and for this reason their capacity to stir up to revenge and violence in a breach of the peace, is vastly increased. For this reason libel was indictable under the common law as the District Attorney said, while slander was never indictable. But the common law did not permit the truth to be given in evidence because, according to Lork Coke, (5 Co. 125) "the greater "appearance there is of truth in any mali- "cious invective, so much the more pro- "voking is it." Lord Mansfield stated the same doctrine in his famous saying " the greater the truth the greater the libel." By your Honors ruling I had almost concluded you held to the same opinion now.

But sir in 6 and 7 Victoria, ch. 96 it is enacted that "truth should be a defence if it was published for the public benefit," or in other words, "through benevolence to the public."

You Honor doubtless remembers the great case of "the people of New York vs Crosswell in 1803. This was an alleged libel of Thomas Jefferson. The question whether the truth could be given in evidence as a defence was ably argued by Alexander Hamilton, then in his prime, on the affirmative but the court was divided, Justices Kent and Thomson agreed with Hamilton, while Lewis and Livingston dissented. The verdict having been against the defendant, and the Court being equally divided, Judgment would have been pronounced, had not the Legislature in 1805 enacted a law declaring "that the truth should be a defence, provided it were published with good motives and for justifiable ends."

Either by constitutional provision, legislative enactment or adjudication of the Courts, this is now the law, in every State in the Union. If I mistake not, in the case of the Commonwealth vs. Daniels, this State took the lead in this reform.

In the case of the State vs. Burnham, 9 N. H. 43, the Supreme Court decided that in a case like this, "If the defendant justified " by 'showing truth' his motives are not in "question. If upon a lawful occasion for " making a publication, he has published the " truth and no more, there is no sound prin- "ciple which can make him liable, even if he " was actuated by express malice." It has " been said that it is lawful to publish truth " from good motives and for justifiable ends. " But this rule is too narrow. If there is a " lawful occasion—a legal right to make a " publication and the matter true, the end is " justifiable.

In the case of the Commonwealth vs. Clapp, 4 Mass. Reports, p. 163. It was held that " the defendant may repel the charge " by proving the publication was for a justi- " fiable purpose and not malicious nor with " the intent to defame any man."

In a medical book like this, privileged under the law, these decisions all go to show it is the duty of the Commonwealth to *prove malice* for it cannot be presumed. The burden of proof is not on this defendant, although we could have shown a total want of malice, had you not kept out our witnesses.

COURT.—I put in substitutes.

MR. KILGORE.—Yes, your Honor put in opinions but you ruled out testimony which would have acquited my client.

We offered to prove that the book was sold only to adult persons—that Dr. Landis did not sell to agents but sold this book ONLY AT HIS OWN OFFICE corner of Girard Avenue and Thirteenth street. We offered to prove that he gave five sixths of his income for the purpose of enlightening the people on this and kindred subjects, during the last year; that the book was calculated to benefit, not demoralize society, that it was a medical work much needed, and not obscene, and you ruled it all out. Your Honor ruled out all our offers to prove the *truth of this publication*, and distinctly charged the jury that it made no difference whether the book was true or false, when the law distinctly says that in case of a privileged communication "the defendant may justify by showing the truth, his motives are not in question." State vs Burnham 9. N. H. 43.

I now come to the fifth reason.

The learned Court erred in charging the Jury in words following to wit: '

"Now, gentlemen, in order to justify, a publication of this character you must be satisfied in your own minds that the publication was made for a legitimate and useful end and purpose; that it was not done from any wanton motive; any motive of mere gain, or with a corrupt desire to debauch society.

These remarks were calculated to make the jury believe that *The Secrets of Generation* was in the same category with the book purchased of Scroggy, on Vine Street next door to the Methodist Church. That book was not designed to do good, it had no redeeming feature, but was only calculated to injure the public. The mere publication of such a work is sufficient evidence from which malice is presumed. But the *Secrets of Generation* occupies entirely different ground.

It was written upon a lawful occasion, by one who "honestly meant" to inform the public mind and "warn them against the dangers in society," and who as a physician and a minister had a legal and moral right to publish it. It is nothing against this defendant that he advertized it for sale in a manner peculiar to himself.

The Doctor believed it calculated to do immense good and in this faith, strove to give it an extensive circulation. There is no law restricting the sale of any medical work neither are such works usually published and circulated free. Authors generally desire their books to yield some pecuniary return and there is no law preventing them from thus earning a livelihood.

That book published in London by Dr. Bell, called "KALOGYNOMIA, or the Laws of Female Beauty" which your Honor complimented so highly, I consider a very improper book to put into the hands of children, when attending school as was mentioned in your charge. That book had one plate representing precisely what Doctor Landis tells married persons should be done, and what the jury called obscene—for they were not out long enough to read more than those passages the District Attorney marked, and although that work was more objectionable as a book for children, it was sold to anybody.

COURT.—Was that sold promiscuously?

MR. KILGORE.—Yes sir—to every body who would buy it. No restriction was put upon its sale because it is a medical work. If Doctor Landis had not been thus careful of the sale of the SECRETS OF GENERATION ; if he had sold it to your children or mine, I do not think the law would punish him. But sir, neither your children nor mine, would so far forget the lessons taught them at home as ever to send for such books by mail. Medical books, proper for adults but improper for children, must be restricted in their circulation by that inate sense of modesty in all minds, and the moral sense of the community, rather than by statute law. There was no evidence of any wrong motive in publishing this book, and the fact that he made millions of dollars by the sale of it would not prove malice. The law says in a case like this—"the burden of proof is on the plaintiff to "satisfy the "jury that the libel was malicious and that " if the plaintiff did not *prove* the malice " beyond a reasonable doubt, that doubt "should be in favor of the defendant." 3 Howards Reports 291.

So when your Honor came to those points of the law, copied *verbatim* from the decisions of the Judges no less renowned than

68

Lord Mansfield and Chief Justice Marshall, and others of more modern times, you so interpreted their language as to destroy the effect they otherwise would have had on behalf of the defendant.

When requested to charge, that "The law "will not presume a communication to have "been through malice, which was made "confidentially in good faith and in discharge "of a legal, social or moral obligation and "through benevolence to the public', You affirmed it, but in such a manner as to rob it of all effect in this case on the minds of the jury. Your Honor said "I affirm this point. The meaning of it is that if you are aware that anybody is doing an injury generally, and you give information respecting it in good faith, and in a proper manner, you are protected. But where this is done for the purpose of gain, for the purpose of making money without regard to the welfare of society and the communication itself tends to excite passion, and provoke obscenity, in such a case the law does not hold."

This, I submit was practically rendering the law inoperative and void, so far as this case is concerned.

The second point was taken from Lord Mansfield's decision in the case of Republica v. Dennie, 4 Brown, 2552. "If the pro-"duction was honestly meant to inform the "public mind and warn them against sup-"posed dangers in society—though the sub-"ject may have been treated erroneously—"then, however the Judgment of the Jury "may decline them to think individually, "they should acquit the defendant. If the "Jury doubt of the criminal intention then "also the law pronounces that he should be "acquitted."

Instead of affirming it as was your duty to do as a Judge, your Honor said "If the publication was proper to be made, that is, gentlemen, if the injury is effected by the publication itself, then no matter how mistaken the party may have been in supposing he was doing good, he is within the law.

It does not do for men to imagine they are doing good, when they are doing things tending to injure and debauch society and to think that they are to be justified in their act because men happen to have a different opinion.'

These remarks from the Court, were not only uncalled for, but I consider them dangerous to liberty. If one judge can thus annul the law in one case, another can do it in some other case equally important, and the time might soon come when well settled

principles in law, favorable to liberty would be used to take from the citizen all civil rights.

The third point of law, that

"A communication made bona fide upon "any subject matter in reference to which "he has a duty, is privileged, if made to a "person having a corresponding duty, "although it contained criminating matter, "which without this privilege would be "slanderous and actionable." Harrison v. Bush, 32 Eng. Law & Eq. 173.

Your Honor neither affirmed nor denied, but made it inapplicable to this case, in the minds of the jury, and applicable to dishonest servants.

The fourth point

"If the use to be attained is justifiable, "as, if the object is generally to give useful "information to the community, or to those "who have a right and ought to know, in "order that they may act upon such infor-"mation, the occasion is lawful and the "party may then justify or excuse the pub-"lication." State v. Burnham. 9 N. H. Rep, shared the same fate.

The fifth point, your Honor was requested to affirm, in your charge to the jury is as follows,

"It is the undoubted right of every mem-"ber of the community to publish his own "opinions on all subjects of public and com-"mon interest, and so long as he exercises "this inestimable privilege candidly, hon-"estly and sincerely with a view to benefit "society he is not amenable as a criminal."

I am willing to risk my reputation upon the truth of the assertion that Doctor Landis honestly and sincerely intended to benefit society by the publication of this book.

Some eighteen or twenty years ago he solemnly dedicated his life to the work of putting a stop to sensuality, immorality and crime, which results from ignorance of these great laws of Nature, which underlie all progress and all reformation. To this great work he has devoted all his energies. His whole life has been a rebuke to sensuality, intemperance and vice. Had we been permitted we could have proved he had the good of Society in view in which case the law says "he is not amenable as a criminal."

Our sixth point,

"If the Jury find the teaching of this "book calculated to benefit the persons to

" whom it is dedicated—they should acquit
" the Defendant."

Your Honor neither affirmed nor denied,
but your language weighed heavily against
this Defendant.

Instead of affirming a well settled principle of the law—you said "Well gentlemen
it may be under peculiar circumstances,
" that a person may derive benefit from the
" book, but placed indiscriminately in the
" hands of persons not requiring such ad-
" vice and benefit and it tends to inflame
" their minds, and is obscene in its character,
" then gentlemen it is not protected.

" It is for you to determine the character
" of the book if in your judgment you think
" the book is fit and proper for the welfare
" of society, and that such a book as that
" ought to be published, and it is such as so-
" ciety demands, and ought to go into
" your families to be handed down to your
" sons and daughters and placed in boarding
" schools, and so forth, for general useful
" information, why then if that be the char-
" acter of the book it is your duty to acquit
" the defendant,"

Court.—The point could not be put
more broadly than that.

Mr. Kilgore.—Yes your Honor, but it
begged the whole question. We proved
by several witnesses that the book had
benefitted them. No "peculiar circumstances" were proven. We proved that
the book was not "placed indiscriminately
in the hands of persons, whether they required such advice or not. It was never
intended for a school book, for boarding
schools or any other schools, but it was a
STRICTLY PRIVATE BOOK FOR MARRIED PER
SONS. He never sold a copy to any person
under eighteen years of age and not then
till satisfied they were about to become
husbands or wives. He never sent a copy
by mail, without being satisfied the party
sending for it was a proper person to have
it, and always sent it under seal. I have
been told on one occasion he gave away a
dozen copies of the book, for proper dis-
tribution, so confidant was he it would do
good: Where people were poor he always
gave them the book, when he thought they
needed its instruction, without money and
without price. His object was not *mere
gain,* but to teach his fellow men to obey
the laws of their own nature.

The seventh point, is the exact language
of well settled principles of the law.

"If the jury believe the defendant had
" in view the benefit of society—however
" wrong the ideas or objectionable the lan-
" guage—there is no malice and he should be
" acquitted," properly affirmed, according to
the book would have acquitted this defendant.

Court.—Suppose the Jappanese should
come here some day, and should perform ba-
kari, on himself, would he be a murderer
or not? How far would his conscience
and his views of propriety protect him?
You might say he was insane.

Mr Kilgore.—I say he could not be
convicted of murder under the law of any
State in the Union.

Court.—I said if you put it upon the
ground of insanity you are all right.

Mr. Kilgore.—When a person believes,
(not always what he professes to believe)
religiously that he should give his child
to the Delaware, as people have been
taught by their priests through all the past,
to sacrifice their children to appease the
wrath of the Great Spirit, (following the
murderous example of Abraham, so much
admired as the father of the faithful, by
christians) giving them to the Ganges, or
the car of Juggernaut; if it were possible for
such a scene to be enacted in Philadelphia
to day from a consciencious belief it was
duty thus to do, no law would hold that
person responsible as a criminal, because
all crime involves a wrong intent.

Such a person would be pronounced by
the law insane, but if the intent was good,
it would be no crime for which the law
would hold him responsible. The law is
directly in conflict with what your Honor
said upon the eighth point, contained in
our fifteenth reason for a new trial. That
" it is not his view as to what will injure
Society, that is to determine his guilt or innocence."

You also said "The whole defence is not
that he was not offering it for sale, but that
he was not offering an obscene book."

This was a gross misstatement of a fact,
which ought to give us a new trial. It is
the right of this defendant, because your
Honor made so great a mistake. There is
a whole avalanche of cases where new

trials have been granted for a much less misdirection of the judge.

COURT.—Do you mean to say that there was a doubt of his having sold the book or offering it for sale?

MR. KILGORE.—No sir. But that Doctor Landis was not offering an obscene book for sale was *not* our whole defence. We took the ground also that the book was what the law terms *privileged*, being a scientific and medical work; that it was written to benefit Society, upon a lawful occasion by a medical man upon a medical subject.

We also took the ground that the book, to those to whom it was addressed and to whom it was sold, was not obscene, but was calculated to do good. All this and more we should have proven had not your Honor, in violation of law as I think, ruled all this testimony out. The District Attorney made a great ado over the obscenity of some few passages of this book. To a person having correct ideas of the sacredness of the generative functions, with a mind uncontaminated by licentiousness, there is nothing obscene in this book, not one single word or sentence contained in it.

I say now, and here before your Honor and before Heaven, that I believe the book to be highly useful and beneficial, that society needs it, and is calling for it by all the diseases, evils and crimes which result from that ignorance this book was intended to banish.

Our sixteenth reason I have already discussed. "If the design of the book was to " benefit society it does not show malice to " take measures to extend its circulation." On this point as on all previous ones, your Honor took the law from this case and applied it to something else.

Not only was the "*Secrets of Generation*" designed to benefit society, but we proved by several witnesses it actually had benefitted people. Your Honor would be surprised to read the letters Doctor Landis has received from persons all over the country as to the benefit received from this book. As I have before remarked, all authors desire their books to be circulated, and advertising it for extensive circulation

does not show malice. Besides I have clearly shown that the law puts the burden of proof of malice upon the Commonwealth, this they have presumed but failed to prove. *The verdict was against the evidence and the weight of the evidence.*

We proved the book had benefitted people by several witnesses and not a person could be found who had ever been injured by it. The jury, therefore, entirely ignored this testimony and convicted this defendant against the evidence.

They paid no attention to the fact, that his character, or rather reputation for purity, amongst those who knew him was good. Why sir, he has been preaching and practicing in this city for the last seventeen years, and we proved he was a minister of religion, and although the District Attorney prayed God to forgive the man who ordained him, I can assure that officer that no forgiveness is needed. Doctor Landis preached one of the best sermons last Sunday night I ever heard from human lips. The trouble is he preaches too much truth, for the Pharisees and Hypocrites of this age, who honor God with their lips while their hearts are far from Him.

Doctor Landis is misunderstood. It is one of the easiest things in the world to be misunderstood. We live in an age, when things are not what they seem, and when any man rebukes the sins of the people he may expect to be misrepresented. Why your Honor knows that however hard you may strive to do justice in your important position as a judge, the newspapers and private individuals often find fault with you. They often censure you when you do right and are ready to flatter you when unintentionally you do wrong. Doctor Landis is a firm believer in the laws of God. He takes Jesus as his exemplar and often says " woe unto you Scribes, Pharisees, and Hypocrites."

He has been rasped by the men in power —wealthy men who have been enriched by gigantic corporations, who now control the Public as well as the private Ledgers of this city. These men have shut him out of their papers, out of public halls and have done all in their power to put him down, simply and only because his daily life is a constant rebuke to their own. Doctor Landis has been a constant advocate of temperance. He believes in the Gospel of personal cleanliness and purity.

He teaches the thousands who flock to hear him, that you cannot honor God in a body debauched by pork, whiskey, drugmedicines or tobacco. He believes in having good muscle, sinew, nerve and bone, and wages perpetual war against all licentiousness and sin. Why sir, on one occasion I saw a minister stop in the midst of his prayer to put a large quid of tobacco in his mouth, and it so shocked me I have never quite recovered from it. He was a fraud. They, who revile this defendant and hold up their hands in horror at the mention of Dr. Landis' name, who pray God to sanctify them while their bodies are filthy and diseased from intemperance, will yet be found unworthy to unloose the latchet of his shoes.

COURT.—You remember the answer of Sojourner Truth when she was asked by a person whether any thing unclean should enter into heaven, answered, "no, I do not expect there will," then said he how do you expect to take your unclean breath there? "Bless your heart," said she, "I expect to leave my breath behind me when I go there."

MR. KILGORE.—True your Honor—but had Sojourner Truth been properly educated she would have known that the spirit is dependant upon the body, and the body is made up in part of what we eat. That tobacco, being one of the most subtle poisons known to man, acting principally upon the *nerves*, which are most closely connected with the spirit, damages the soul as well as the body through the close sympathy between them. That the body is the souls dwelling place, and should be kept so pure that it may be a fit temple for the holy (or whole) ghost to dwell in.

In the case of the Commonwealth v. Twitchell, 1 Brewster's Reports, 609, it has been decided by this Court, that a new trial should be granted in a case which will bear this threefold test, viz:

1. Was there any evidence to justify the verdict?

2. Is it clearly against the weight of the testimony?

3. Is there any reasonable hope that another trial would produce a different result?

In regard to the first question, I answer emphatically, NO.

No witness called the SECRETS OF GENERATION obscene. The jury decided this case not by the evidence, but by the statement of the District Attorney and upon your Honor's opinion.

I think, the verdict was clearly against the weight of the testimony, as I have before shown. Could we have a new trial, I do not believe there is another jury to be found in Philadelphia that would convict this defendant.

THE VERDICT WAS AGAINST THE LAW.

On this point I have spoken throughout this argument, and therefore have but one word to say. The law permits us to examine experts. This was refused.

COURT.—Have you found any one case at all in which a charge of this character was made, where experts were admitted?

MR. KILGORE.—There is no case on record, I think, where a medical book like this, sold under seal, which the law has privileged for the last three hundred years, by the decisions of Coke, Ellenborough and Mansfield, and by nearly all the decisions to which I referred, was ever attempted to be restrained by such a proceeding as this. Some few years ago, the attempt was made in New York by an ignorant detective to restrain the circulation of this very book, but as soon as the judge saw it, he pronounced it a medical work, privileged by law, and dismissed the complaint.

COURT.—What would be the influence of a medical work if it had been put in the hands of a young daughter, or in the hands of one of tender years, would it not be obscene then? Take such a book as you produce here, put it into the hands of a person of tender years, without any expression of opinion as to the intention, what would be the effect?

MR. KILGORE.—I would not like to have any one place such a work in the hands of a child, too young to know of physiology. A man who would place either of the medical works we produced here, illustrated with plates, in the hands of a child too young to know of Anatomy, would do very wrong, but the man who would place the book bought of Scroggy in the hands of any one, old or young, would be deserving of the scorn of all decent men and should go to the penitentiary besides.

COURT.—I put that case to show that a book may be an obscene libel in improper hands.

MR. KILGORE.—That we admit your Honor. But shall we destroy all scientific and medical works which are useful in proper hands because they would do harm to children?

I pray you to make this case your own. The real enemies to the morals of this community are not those who strive to persuade the people to obey the laws of their Creator, either with voice or pen— neither are they found in the lowest depths of vice in Bedford Street, so ably described by your Honor in charging the Grand Jury a few weeks ago.

The men of leisure and idleness, called *gentlemen*, who live in palaces and luxury and have money to keep mistresses and live lives of prostitution, are the real enemies of morality and virtue in this community.

I know the District Attorney is greatly prejudiced against my client, yet if he could know all the facts respecting Doctor Landis, which have come to me, I believe he would lose his prejudice and agree with me, that this is a PERSECUTION rather than a prosecution. He would agree with me that it would be an outrage against justice and against the law, to sentence this defendant under the present verdict.

Therefore I pray him and I pray your Honor, to remember this defendant as though you yourselves were in his place, and I think the District Attorney will show nobility in nothing so much, as in being generous and magnanimous to the man who has been so poorly defended.

COMMON PLEAS.

COMMONWEALTH vs. S. M. LANDIS.

New Trial—Evidence.

Opinion by PIERCE, J. Jan. 22, 1870.

The reasons for a new trial in this case are numerous, but they may all be disposed of under a few heads. They relate:

FIRST.—To the exclusion of evidence tending to show the scientific correctness of the book complained of, and the fitness of such a publication for general information.

SECOND.—To an expression of opinion by the Judge as to the character of the book.

THIRD.—To errors in charging the jury as to what constituted an obscene libel, and as to what extent a publication is protected as necessary for general information and conducive to the public welfare.

1. Physicians were called as experts to show the scientific correctness of the book and the necessity of such knowledge for general information.

I ruled at the trial that the book might be true and scientifically correct in its statements and descriptions, and yet be obscene; that its obscenity did not depend upon its truthfulness or falsity, but upon its tendency to inflame the passions and debauch society. The character of the book was a question purely for the jury, in which they could not be aided by the testimony of experts. Obscenity is determined by the common sense and feelings of mankind, and not by the skill of the learned. It was therefore a question for the jury, to be determined by their examination of the publication, and not by the opinions of others respecting it. That which offends modesty, and is indecent and lewd, and tends to the creation of lascivious desires, is obscene. Of this the jury were as competent to judge as the most accomplished experts in medical science, whose familiarity with the subjects treated of in the book might, perhaps, render them less susceptible to the emotions which would be excited in the general public by reading such a book.

2. Relative to the expression of opinion by the Judge as to the character of the book, it was held by the Supreme Court in Kilpatrick v. The Commonwealth. 7 Casey, 198, that a Judge may rightfully express his opinion respecting the evidence and it may sometimes be his duty to do it, yet not so as to withdraw it from the consideration and decision of the jury.

My own experience as a Judge has taught me that it is sometimes not only expedient but necessary to the proper administration of law and justice that a Judge should express his opinion on the evidence submitted to the jury. His greater familiarity with the rules of evidence. the weight of the testimony, and its application to its subject-matter of investigation, requires that he should do so; but he should always accompany it with the instruction, that the facts of the case are for their determination. under the evidence submitted to them.

In this case this instruction was repeated to the jury more than once. They were told that they were not to take my opinion of the book, but were to determine its character from their own examination of it. Again, they were instructed that it was for them to determine the character of the book. If in their judgment the book was fit and proper for publication, and such as should go into their families and be handed to their sons and daughters, and placed in boarding schools for the beneficial information of the young, and others, then it was their duty to acquit the defendant.

They were further instructed that if they had a doubt as to the obscenity of the book it was their duty to acquit the defendant.

This instruction left the whole question of the character of the publication to the jury. There was no controversy as to the publication of the book by the defendant, as its publication was substantially, if not in terms, admitted by him.

3. The next alleged error relate to the charge of the court as to what constitutes an obscene libel, and to what extent a publication is protected as necessary for general information and conducive to the public welfare.

The jury were instructed that it did not matter whether the things published in the book were true, and in conformity with nature and the laws of our being or not. If to inflame improper and lewd passions, it was an obscene libel. That to justify a publication of the character of the book, they must be satisfied that the publication was made for a legitimate and useful purpose, and that it was not made from any motive of mere gain, or with a corrupt desire to debauch society. That even scientific and medical publications containing illustrations exhibiting the human form, if wantonly exposed in the open markets, with a wanton and wicked desire to create a demand for them, and not to promote the good of society by placing them in proper hands for useful purposes, would, if tending to excite lewd desires, be held to be obscene libels.

That before a medical class, for the purpose of instruction, it might be necessary and proper, and consonant with decency and modesty, to expose the human body for exhibition of disease, or for the purpose of operation, but that if the same human body were exposed in front of one of our medical colleges to the public indiscriminately, even for the purpose of operation, such an exhibition would be held to be indecent and obscene.

The jury were further instructed that publications of this character are protected when made with a view to benefit society, and in a manner not to injure the public, but that a mistaken view of the defendant as to the character and tendency of the book, if it was in itself obscene and unfit for publication, would not excuse his violation of the law.

After having listened to the elaborate and earnest argument of the learned counsel for the defendant, I do not perceive that there was error either in the admission or exclusion of evidence, or in charge to the jury, and I think that the verdict is sustained by both the law and the evidence. The motion for a new trial is therefore overruled.

REMARKS OF THE JUDGE.

The offence of which you have been convicted, is one, which to my mind, is of a grievous character. I know nothing, which of itself, tends more to the demoralization of society, and to the corruption of pure minds, and especially of the young, than a publication of the character of which you have been convicted.

It should be the desire of every one in a community like this, or whether the community be great or small, to hold the minds, not only of the mature, but of the young, pure and untainted, and anything which tends to break down the natural modesty and purity of the human mind is subversive of the highest interests of our being.

I think that the law has affixed to the offence of which you have been convicted, a mild penalty.

I know of cases, of civil cases, in which it would be my duty, if the law warranted it in extending the term of imprisonment which is provided by the act of assembly, therefore, though I believe it my duty to impose upon you the full sentence provided by the act of assembly, still I feel it is but reasonable in itself.

SENTENCE.

The sentence of the court is, therefore, that you pay a fine of FIVE HUNDRED DOLLARS, *and undergo an imprisonment in the Philadelphia County Prison* FOR THE TERM OF ONE YEAR.

PHILADELPHIA, January 22, 1870

PRAYER

TO, AND FOR, THE PEOPLE!

Written in Moyamensing Prison at Philadelphia, Pa., February 4th. 1870.

By DR. S. M. LANDIS, The Progressive Christian.

Let all the Earth keep silence, before Thee—Thou unchangeable Creator of all things. Thou, who has fixed Thy laws from the foundation of the world, we rejoice in Thy Glory. We Love Thee, because Thou art *not* partial! We appreciate Thy infallible fidelity to Thine own handiwork, and we pray Thee, sent down, *direct from heaven,* Thy magnetizing and inspiring influences and baptize this people with similar fidelity and sound sense; that, they may give themselves up to Thy fixed laws, thereby receive the Spirit of Christ Jesus!

And, *now,* O, Lord! I, Thy humble prisoner, do *most* devoutly pray all THE PEOPLE of Thy footstool to behold Thy magnificent and immutable injunctions, and yield, a cheerful obeisance, to Thy words and works as holily inscribed upon Thy "Book of Nature;" and as most beautifully and logically consummated by the faithful Nazarene, who came *not* with gaudy trappings and worldly clamor; but, who linked himself into Thy Laws and Works, thereby giving *the people* the exemplification of power and grace divine!

Lord God, Father of All, Thou who hast made everything for the good, the health, the normal prosperity, the happiness and everlasting bliss of *all* people; I, therefore, most heartily beseech *them* to appreciate this infallible token of Thy LOVE for them! Moreover, as Thou hast designed that they should have dominion over the things of earth; so likewise, I *invoke them* to accept Thy proffered promises by upholding Thy Laws and Handiwork as *alone* supreme!

O, Thou! Great Jehovah, impress upon their minds the necessity of striking terror to the hearts of haughty *vipers*, who usurp power, which *alone* belongs to Thee, and which Thou has vouchsafed unto Thy obedient sovereign people! Yea, teach them that the fixed "*Laws of Nature*" are Thy creation; hence, all rules or laws instituted by men must be in harmony with *Thy* laws and works, otherwise they are a bugbear and stumbling-block to Grace Divine!

Father of Mercies, to gain Salvation, teach them the incumbent duty to return to truth and nature; and to "prevent the ills that flesh is heir to," by observing Thy fixed laws of the "SECRETS OF GENERATION," (as truthfully and honestly expressed in that *book* for which Thy humble servant *now* suffers imprisonment, at the hands of incompetent and lewd persons). thereby striking at the *root* of evil, when the unborn generations, will have the *Image of God* stamped upon their countenances, (instead of the mark of Cain) and will intuitively praise Thy holy name, by words and deeds, forever and ever! Amen.

APPENDIX.

———•••———

PHILADELPHIA, MONDAY January 10, 1870.
I have read the "Secrets of Generation" 18 mo. Philadelphia 1866, pages 36, by S. M. Landis M. D. D. D. and I cannot discover anything I think obscene or demoralizing.
JAMES McCLINTOCK, M. D.
823 RACE STREET.
Sworn and Subscribed before me this 10th day of January, 1870.
WM. P. HIBBARD, ALDERMAN. [*Seal*]

This may certify that I have read the "Secrets of Generation" by S. M. Landis M. D. for married persons or those about to marry. To such persons there is nothing in it obscene, and the information is calculated to benefit mankind.
PHILADELPHIA, February 17, 1870.
JOS. H. NORTH, M. D.

D. Y. KILGORE, ESQ.,
Dear Sir: At your request, I take pleasure in giving my testimony in regard to what I believe to be the motives of S. M. Landis, M. D., in publishing the book entitled " The Secrets of Generation," and his general course in promoting a much needed reform in the social relations of life, and especially so far as the needs and diseases of woman are concerned; and that they were of the purest character—and further I believe he was influenced by his highest sense of duty and his obligations to God and the race.
JOS. S. LONGSHORE, M. D.
1430 NORTH 11TH STREET.
PHILADELPHIA February 28, 1870.